# Free Flight

**PublicAffairs**
*New York*

# · · · · Free Flight

## From Airline Hell
## to a New Age of Travel

*James Fallows*

*Book design by Mark McGarry, Texas Type & Book Works.*
*Set in Meridien.*

The images throughout this book were provided courtesy of the following: Gerry Mengo, p. 24; Cirrus Design Corporation, pp. 33, 40, 43, 92, 95, 97, 98, 111, 115, 123, 124, 125, 134; NASA, pp. 110, 226; Eclipse Aviation, pp. 163, 192; Williams International, pp. 167, 172, 178; Tad Fallows, p. 213; and Deb Fallows, p. 217.

Library of Congress Cataloging-in-Publication Data
Fallows, James M.
Free flight: from airline hell to a new age of travel / James Fallows.—1st ed.
p. cm.
Includes index.
ISBN 1–58648–040–5
1. Airlines—United States. 2. Airlines—Technological innovations—United States. 3. Air travel—United States. I. Title.
HE9803.A4 F35 2001
387.7'0973—dc21
2001019631

FIRST EDITION
10 9 8 7 6 5 4 3 2 1

*For Deb,*
*The original Seven-One-One-Delta-Zulu,*

*And for her parents,*
*Angie and Frank Zerad*

# Contents

# Acknowledgments

I will always be grateful to Ken Michelsen, a former marine pilot and a born teacher, for enduring "primary flight training" as my instructor. The steel nerves he displayed as he sat calmly in the right-hand seat of the cockpit, while the novice pilot in the left seat tried to learn how to land the plane, may have matched anything demanded of him in uniform. I am also very grateful to Chris Baker for training me in instrument flying and in handling the Cirrus SR20, and for instruction in spin recovery and basic aerobatics. Chris Jacobs gave me delightful lessons in flying pontoon planes in the Puget Sound. Gary Black, a former navy flier, introduced me to the way truly modern planes perform when we flew in a Cirrus from the Los Angeles area to Duluth in 1999.

Warren Morningstar, of the Aircraft Owners and Pilots Association, nudged me out of indecision with a demo flight when I was not sure about starting flying lessons. Peter Pathe was a wonderful flying companion in Seattle. Others who have shared their enthusiasm for the subject include Dick Anderegg, Sharon and Damon Darlin, Julian Fischer, Tom Gibson, Eric and Heather Redman, Peter Rinearson, Sam Howe Verhovek, and Joe Yap.

The founders of the military reform movement of the early 1980s, Chuck Spinney, Pierre Sprey, and above all the late John Boyd, originally drew my interest to the question of how advanced technology could make airplanes faster, cheaper, safer, and simpler to operate, rather than ever more expensive and breakdown-prone. In my book *National Defense* I discussed the way this logic applied to military aircraft. In a sense the people I describe in *Free Flight* are civilian counterparts to those military reformers.

In Duluth and at Cirrus Design I appreciate the time, generosity, and cooperation of Kate Dougherty-Andrews, Lisa Bath, Ian Bentley, Tom Bergeron, Gary Black and Celeste Curley-Black, Cindy Brown, Mike Busch, Tom Cotruvo, Mayor Gary Doty, Paul Johnston, Alan and Dale Klapmeier, Chris Maddy, Tom Shea, Mike van Staagen, Pat Waddick, and others. Laurie Anderson was generous in talking about her late husband Scott.

At Williams International and Eclipse Aviation I spoke with many people and especially appreciate the help of Cory Canada, Dottie Hall, Oliver Masefield, and Vern Raburn. At NASA I am grateful for the time and help of Steve Campbell, Keith Henry, and especially Bruce Holmes. Tom Bowen of the Mooney Aircraft Corporation generously spent a day showing me how the fast, rugged Mooneys are built.

I benefited greatly from the comments that Lincoln Caplan, Garrett Gruener, Rich Karlgaard, Kevin Moore, Eric Schmidt, and Lawrence Wilkinson made on an earlier version of this book. At PublicAffairs, Peter Osnos, Robert Kimzey, and their colleagues produced the book with remarkable calm, agility, and skill. I had worked with William Whitworth for many years at the *Atlantic Monthly* and was delighted to have his counsel as editor of this book. My agent Wendy Weil was once again of great help. At the *Atlantic*, Michael Kelly, Corby Kummer, Cullen Murphy, Sue Parilla, Martha Spaulding, Wen Stephenson, Barbara Wallraff, and others helped me complete this project and generally made it a daily pleasure to be part of their enterprise. Katherine Bouton and Adam Moss of the *New York Times Magazine* encouraged me on an early version of the Cirrus Design story. I revised the book using a new version of Microsoft Word, for which I was on the product planning team early in 1999. I am grateful to all members of the Word development team for the new editing features they built in. I organized the research material for this book using an ingenious program called Zoot. I greatly admire its creator, Tom Davis of Lincoln, Vermont, and hope that others will try his product at www.zootsoftware.com.

As always, my main debt is to my family: my wife, Deb; our sons, Tom and Tad; and our parents, Jean and James A. Fallows of Redlands, California, and Angie and Frank Zerad of Englewood, Florida.

Berkeley, California

# Free Flight

# Introduction: Overload

On a warm, breezy day in September, I took off in a little pro-peller-driven plane from Oakland's international airport. I was headed east, toward Boston, and my wife and twenty-year-old son were aboard. The excuse for this journey was to take our son from California, where we were living, back east for his third year of college. The real reason was to see how the whole country looked from inside a little airplane.

A few years earlier, I had satisfied a long-held curiosity about what it would be like to learn to fly. About a year before this flight, I had with tortured logic talked the rest of the family into accepting the "convenience" of having a small plane of our own. With our older son already out of college, most of our tuition-paying years were behind us. The house was paid off; I was nearing age fifty and wouldn't be getting any younger; having a plane would let us travel and see unusual sights. The new plane I had ordered was not yet ready when we made this coast-to-coast trip, so we had arranged to use instead a demo from the factory.

The nature of the airplane to which I had decided to devote so much money and entrust my family's safety is an important part of the story this book has to tell. It is significant because it is the first sign of an impending, potentially broad change in the choices the traveling public has for getting quickly and conveniently from place to place. But before saying more about this plane, and the related developments in aviation whose effects the public will soon feel, I need to acknowledge the differences between two cultures of the aviation world. I think of them as the Enthusiasts and the Civilians.

Aviation enthusiasts are pilots, people who wish they were pilots, model-aircraft builders, and others who think there is romance in the air. For enthusiasts, anything that flies is interesting in itself. Their biggest tribal gathering is the AirVenture convention, sponsored by the Experimental Aircraft Association and held each summer in Oshkosh, Wisconsin. More than half a million people attend each show; ten thousand or so arrive in their own planes, park on huge meadows, and set up tents next to their machines. Then, for more than a week, they wander through displays of every sort of airplane, old and new, large and small. Enthusiasts have always been a tiny minority. In 2000, just under 700,000 Americans were licensed pilots, or roughly one quarter of 1 percent. Enthusiasts in general and pilots in particular are nearly all men. As long as records have been kept, the proportion of pilots who are women has been between 5 and 10 percent.

Enthusiasts often say that they have "always" been interested in flying, and many have made economically irrational decisions in order to be involved with airplanes as a career. Licensed pilots as a group are less chichi and rich than the image of private planes would suggest. Some are professionals or successful businessmen who can buy their way into the fancier class of plane. A generation ago, the standard example would be the flying doctor or dentist; now it would be the flying software engineer. But many other pilots—most, in my experience—are far from wealthy. They learned to fly when they were young, or perhaps in the military during the Korean War through Vietnam War eras. Now they use their money to rent airplanes, or to maintain old ones, rather than to buy a better house or nicer car. The typical gathering of pilots is like an RV or hot rod–enthusiasts' club. People have grease under their fingernails. The aircraft business is littered with stories of start-up companies that failed. One important reason is that, as with wineries or small country inns or literary magazines, people have tried to start businesses because they loved the activity, not because they necessarily had a good business plan.

Civilians—meaning most of the rest of us—view airplanes not as fascinating objects but as transportation. Planes are better than cars, buses, or trains to the extent that they are faster. Over the last generation, most civilians have learned to assume that large airliners nearly always take off and land safely. For every nervous flyer, there is a crowd of surrounding seatmates ready with explanations that airlines are statistically the safest way to get from point to point. The occasional horrific exception is all the more terrifying because there is no pattern or predictability to it. But civilians view small planes with deep mistrust. The fact that they fly closer to the ground, and are more likely to get bumped around by the winds, is an unalloyed negative. From the civilian perspective, the bigger the plane, the better. Most civilians view people who fly small planes the way I view people who bungee-jump or climb Mount Everest: they are nuts. The main way the small-plane culture enters general consciousness is with the stories of the latest politician, athlete, or celebrity who has died in a crash.

I am a civilian who has gotten a look at the enthusiast world. For the last few years I have read about small airplanes, spent time in small airplanes, gotten to know people who have devoted their lives to this pursuit. Because of these excursions I've come to know about certain pockets of the enthusiast culture that are destined to change life for civilian travelers. Changes in aviation technology have often originated in just this way. From the Wright brothers onwards, many of the people who have invented systems that affect the way the general public travels have themselves been part of the small minority obsessed with flying machines. The exception illustrating the rule, a civilian who profoundly changed the nature of travel for other civilians, is Alfred Kahn. He was the economist from Cornell who, in the late seventies, oversaw the deregulation of airline prices and schedules. For better and worse Kahn introduced the airline system of today.

The topic of this book is the problem civilians face: namely, the inefficient hell that modern airline travel has become. But to explain the ingenious, emerging solutions to that problem requires an excursion into the world of the enthusiasts. Most of this book will concern the experiments the enthusiasts are carrying out and the challenges they have overcome, but the end point is what it will mean for civilians.

Let us start with the civilian problem. People who travel on airlines all have stories about how bad the experience is when things go wrong: lost or damaged luggage; unexplained waits on the taxiway, with the passengers strapped in but the plane not allowed to take off; missed connections and overnight delays because of snow in Denver or fog in San Francisco or thunderstorms in the Midwest.

But the more impressive fact is how unpleasant and wasteful the experience can be when nothing in particular has gone wrong. The series of waits in line: to get through the bridge or tunnel or toll booth to the airport; to drop off the rental car or catch the shuttle bus from the parking lot; to make it to the check-in counter; to pass through the security gate; to get the shuttle to the remote terminal; to buy coffee or sandwiches to supplement the pretzels offered as food on the trip; to get onto the plane itself and join the fight for space in the overhead bins. Because any of these intermediate dead-waits can turn out to be much longer than "normal," worst-case padding for all of them must be built into plans for leaving home or work for the airport. As flight delays reached record levels in the summer of 2000, an executive from an airplane company told me that he'd made a bet with a friend. The bet concerned how long it would be until an argument over cancelled flights or lost bags led one frustrated person to kill another in an airport. It would have happened already, the man said, except that security gates in airports keep passengers from bringing in guns.

Then on the other end, a further series of waits: for the bags; for the car or taxi; for the travel time from the airport to the home, office, meeting, or vacation site you're actually trying to reach. The final leg of the trip, from airport to real destination, can be a minor factor for those traveling nonstop from one airline hub-city to another—New York to Chicago, Atlanta to Dallas-Fort Worth. It represents a very large share of the total travel time for those either beginning or ending their journey somewhere other than one of these big hubs. Time-and-motion studies conducted by NASA in the late nineties found that for trips of 500 miles or less, which includes the majority of air journeys, going by commercial airline was effectively no faster than driving a car. These studies were part of NASA's little-publicized efforts through the nineties to devise solutions for the country's air-transport problems. "Think about it," the administrator of NASA, Daniel Goldin, said in a speech in 1998. "You are flying through the air at 300 to 500 miles per hour during the part of your trip that is in the commercial airplane. But your *average* speed from when you left your home to when you arrive at your destination is only fifty or sixty miles per hour."[1] When traveling from Oshkosh, where I'd attended my first AirVenture convention, to Seattle, in the summer of 2000, it took me twice as long to get to Chicago's O'Hare Airport, by rented car, as it did to fly from Chicago to Seattle. I could have saved time by taking a commuter plane from Green Bay or Appleton to O'Hare, but with hub-and-spoke pricing my fare to Seattle would have tripled. Every modern traveler has a comparable tale.

The steep pricing penalty for last-minute bookings and changes helps the airlines use their fleets efficiently, as does hub-and-spoke routing itself. But both mean less flexibility and freedom for the traveler. They have also put air travel distinctly out of phase with the evolution of the modern economy as a whole.

Since at least the early nineties, the trend in most businesses and services has been toward on-demand, always-available products and services that fit themselves to the customer's schedule rather than the reverse. You can make or receive phone calls from almost anywhere. You can get money at any time from any ATM in almost any part of the world, and you can do your banking at 3 A.M. on your home computer rather than queuing up for a teller during bankers' hours. You can order books, clothes, or movies by phone, website, or fax and have them delivered as soon as you want. The rising companies of the computing and Internet era in one way or another all made it easier for customers to control and conserve their time: The round-the-clock news networks, so you didn't have to wait for the evening news. Dell, Compaq, and Gateway computers, which let you order just the machine you wanted rather than choosing what happened to be in the store. The booming industry of wireless phones, pagers, and Internet services, which in theory let people make contact with whomever they wanted wherever they were.

Through most of the twentieth century, commercial air travel was an important part of the movement toward giving individuals more freedom, flexibility, and control over how they used their time. In the forties, airplanes first allowed people to go across the country in one long day of travel, rather than eighty hours by train. In the sixties touring families and students could get to Europe on overnight charter flights, rather than spending five days on a ship. Businesses could receive timely shipments from far-off suppliers and coordinate work among offices in different states or countries.

But starting in the nineties, commercial airlines were adding more rigidity than flexibility to the national transportation system. More and more of all traffic flowed through a small number of hub airports. The United States has some 18,000 "landing facilities," including small heliports, and about 5,000 that would be suitable for all but the largest planes.[2] But more than 80 percent of all airline traffic takes off from or lands at the busiest 1 percent of the total—the fifty largest airports and especially the two dozen major "hubs." As the hubs—Dallas, Dulles, Denver, O'Hare, Charlotte, Pittsburgh, Cincinnati, and others—become increasingly saturated with passengers and airplanes, there is that much less give in the system if anything goes wrong. One cancelled flight means passengers sitting in the hallways and filling the standby lists for the subsequent flights. Weather delays in one part of the country have ripple effects thousands of miles away.

"As airline delays get longer, there are more shops and food courts in the terminal," an official of NASA pointed out in the summer of 2000. "Now to truly compare trip costs, you need to include the price for eating and shopping in the airport malls!"[3] McCarran Airport in Las Vegas installed a twenty-four-hour fitness center where stranded passengers could work out. At San Francisco's airport, twenty-seven new restaurants opened during 2000, because of demand from travelers killing time between planes.[4] The structure of fares and the predictability of unpredictable problems meant that people had to tailor their timing and their travel plans to what the airlines offered, in contrast to what they found with other parts of the modern economy.

Helpfully, here too there is an exception proving the rule. Those who can pay enough for first-class seats and last-minute tickets can come closer to fitting travel to their own schedules. And those who can pay the manyfold multiples of first class fare necessary to amortize the cost of a corporate jet can see airplanes as the miracles of freedom they originally were. One springtime evening when I was living in Seattle, I ended up taking a ride in a ten-passenger jet owned by a software billionaire who was going to Monterey, California, for a dinner meeting—and back the same night. He and I and one other guest bound for the dinner left Seattle around five, spent two hours in the air each way, flown by a team of two professional pilots, and were back after dinner a little past midnight. This was freedom and flexibility indeed, only underscoring how different the same journey would have been in normal circumstances. The fastest connection via scheduled airlines, with a change in San Francisco, would have meant leaving Seattle at 1 P.M. and getting back at noon the next day. But private jets like this had cost well over $10 million, and the direct operating costs for the trip were at least $10,000, not counting the pilots' pay.

Of course it seems petty and unfair to complain about modern aircraft or airline companies. When everything goes smoothly—no lines, no delays, no behemoth in the seat ahead reclining into your lap—it can seem miraculous to be transported so far so fast. And despite occasional catastrophic crashes, the airlines' overall safety and reliability are astonishing. During calendar year 1998, absolutely the safest way you could spend time in the United States was as a passenger on a big airplane. In that year, not one person died on a scheduled flight on a U.S. airline, compared with more than one hundred people a day dying in car crashes and about twenty a day in household falls. The previous year, in 1997, a total of two people had died in crashes of U.S.-based airlines.

There have been few dramatic changes in large-aircraft design since the sixties, when both the Concorde and the Boeing 747 made their debuts. But through generation after generation of new models and revisions, planes from Boeing and Airbus have become ever more efficient, more reliable, less polluting, quieter. Airline pilots may sound like corny travel guides when they come onto the intercom, and through the vast majority of a flight they do little more than monitor the airplane's engine gauges, autopilots, and moving-map displays of where the craft is heading. But to have any experience at all with the world of flying is to respect the experience, judgment, and training airline pilots must accumulate before taking their jobs. No other group of professionals is retrained and retested so frequently to be sure they are still mentally and physically up to their tasks. Airline pilots must pass a physical exam, complete with EKG, every six months, and go through no-nonsense retraining at least once a year. An oddly compelling book called *The Black Box* consists of little more than cockpit transcripts from flights that encountered serious trouble.[5] In most cases, the planes crashed and everyone died; in a few, the pilots brought them in with minimal damage. In virtually all the cases, the competence of the crews as they tried to cope with disaster must be called heroic.

How can a system be so technically advanced and admirable, yet lead to results so unpleasant for everyone involved? The explanation is not a paradox or mystery but rather the natural consequence of a recent course of technological development, which itself is about to change. For more than a generation, the money, effort, and innovation in civilian aviation have gone toward planes that can carry one hundred passengers or more between Atlanta and Chicago, New York and Los Angeles, or any other "hub pair," at over 400 miles an hour, with ever-higher reliability and ever-lower cost per mile. While Boeing and Airbus have fought for this market, airplane makers like Gulfstream, Lear, Challenger, Raytheon, and Cessna have poured effort and money into developing ever-faster and sleeker jets that can take corporate officials or individual millionaires wherever they want to go whenever they want to go there. In the history of transportation, the result is like a land-travel system consisting of long-distance rail lines for most passengers and private limousines for a tiny elite. A transportation system, that is to say, like one without the ordinary automobile.

Or to use an analogy from information technology, the last few decades of progress in aviation have meant what the fifties and sixties meant for computing: tremendous advances at the big-ticket, big-iron, corporate-owned level, with little development of low-cost devices that individuals could tailor to their schedules and needs. The result is a system that, much more so than the giant, centralized computers of the sixties, is nearing the limits of its capacity. Only so many airplanes can land at LaGuardia or take off from LAX within a space of sixty minutes. As of 2001, twenty-six of the major hub airports were officially classified as "saturated." That is, they were working at or very close to their maximum capacity. Federal officials predicted in the fall of 2000 that overall airline traffic in the United States would double by 2010, with most of the increase occurring in the twenty-eight already-busiest airports.[6]

What could relieve the overload and change the unpleasant realities of travel? I believe that one answer is being invented by the people whose stories will be told here. They are aviation enthusiasts at small start-up companies, allied with enthusiasts within the federal and state governments, who are trying to create new systems as an alternative to airlines. The governmental role is less surprising than it might initially seem, in light of the federal government's century-long history of support for aviation, including serving as a crucial early customer for the Wright Brothers. But in this case, contrary to the pattern in most twentieth-century defense contracting, the government is dealing with new, tiny companies and trying to help them innovate without making them into mini defense contractors who will remain permanently dependent on its funds.

Eventually these projects should make it possible for many people, much of the time, to travel the way a few very rich people do now: in greater comfort, without fighting their way to and from the crowded hubs, leaving from the small airport that's closest to their home or office and flying direct to the small airport closest to where they really want to go. And this would be possible because of a product now missing from the vast array of flying devices: small planes that offer much of the speed, and as much as possible of the safety, of the big airliners, but at a small fraction of the cost of today's corporate jets. With these planes, a minority of enthusiasts could fly themselves, and the civilian majority could hire piloted air-taxi services, and both groups could go direct to their intended destination, at their own schedule, at a cost no higher than today's coach fares. The existence of automobiles changed the individual's options for travel, compared with what they had been when the choices were railroad or horse-drawn wagon. The existence first of computers, then of mobile computers, then of cell phones and wireless devices of all sorts, changed everything about communications. The existence of new traveling machines will change many things—mainly how much time people must waste on their journeys. The creation of those machines is underway.

The two companies I will say most about are the Cirrus Design Corporation, of Duluth, Minnesota, and Eclipse Aviation, of Albuquerque, New Mexico. Cirrus was the first company to begin large-scale production of a genuinely new small airplane, which it called the SR20. This was the plane that I decided to buy, and in which I took my wife and son coast to coast. Eclipse was the company moving fastest toward production of a jet plane priced at well under $1 million, versus at least three or four times that much for all competitors. Eclipse's idea was that these jets, produced by the thousands, could serve as the backbone for a nationwide air-taxi fleet. The first plane is scheduled for delivery in 2003.

These are not the only companies scrambling to change the nature of air travel. The Lancair Company, of Bend, Oregon, has designed a plane similar to Cirrus's, but more powerful and more expensive. The Safire Aircraft Company, of West Palm Beach, Florida, has promised to market a jet plane like the Eclipse. Many other electronics and parts firms, including Avidyne, Garmin, the avionics divisions of B.F. Goodrich and United Parcel Service, and a score of others, are designing new components for the new aircraft. But as of 2001, Cirrus and Eclipse had financial and other advantages that put them ahead in their respective categories. At the moment they are leading the race to change the nature of travel.

Because all of these firms grow out of the enthusiast culture, and are led by people who "always" were interested in airplanes, let me now try to explain, from an admittedly civilian perspective, how the life of the sky could become so captivating.

# Visual Romance

When I was growing up in Southern California in the fifties and sixties, I had no more or less than the typical boy's interest in airplanes. My brother and I made and painted Revell models of the great bombers of World War II. I snapped together balsa-wood gliders and went to the park to watch them fly. I was thrilled when, as a ten-year-old going to Philadelphia from my home in California for a summer visit with my grandparents, I got to take a ride back on what I remember as having been the first jet departure from the Philadelphia airport, a TWA liner that went nonstop to Los Angeles International. In Boy Scouts, I worked for a merit badge that involved going to the local air force base and getting a lecture on thrust-to-weight and lift-to-drag.

But that was about the end of it. My father, who had been trained as a navy doctor, had been undecided when he went into the recruiting office after graduating from high school in 1943. Should he accept a scholarship for medical training via the navy's V-12 program—or become a Marine Corps fighter pilot? When he told his children about this choice, in the fifties, we looked at each other and thought: *choice?* Of course he did the sensible thing! A good steady profession, versus the risk of going down in flames. When I went to college, I saw a "learn to fly" ad in the registration-week newspaper. I took a bus fifteen miles to the nearest airfield to see about lessons, but for reasons of time and money it was obviously impractical, and I never went back.

I got married just after I left college, and had children not long after that. There was no time or money to spend learning to fly. Still I was surprised when I noticed the way I snapped to attention when I heard that someone I met knew how to fly airplanes. I even remember perusing Prince Charles's biography, at the time of his wedding to Diana, and thinking "lucky guy" at one point. It was not so much that he would get to rule an island kingdom or wear his fancy clothes. Rather what I noticed was that as part of his all-round training for kingship he had been sent to flight school.

When our children grew and began to need less of my wife's and my attention, and when, for a two-year period starting in 1996, I had a "regular" office job as a magazine editor, I decided it was time to act. This was the first job I'd had where the "weekend" was a recognized concept. A writer, like most other self-employed people, basically should always be at work, but now, after the magazine went to press very late on Friday nights, there was not much work I had to do on Saturdays. So I went out to the local airport—Montgomery Airpark, in Gaithersburg, Maryland, twenty miles north of Washington, D.C.—and began taking lessons with a former marine pilot named Ken Michelsen.

The first time I went there, I had a shock that is connected to one theme of this book. The machines were so *cruddy*. I was later to learn that practically no small planes have been built since the late seventies. Twenty years later, they ran better than twenty-year-old cars, because of rigid requirements for maintenance. But they didn't look any better, inside or out, than a twenty-year-old

Gremlin or Montego would. The first few lessons were in freezing January conditions, in which I had to scrape frost off creaky aluminum wings. I thought: this is less fun than I'd hoped.

But on "I've waited this long" principles, I kept trying. I stayed with the lessons, got my private pilot's certificate while in Washington, and got my instrument rating while my wife and I were living in Seattle in 1999. Later that year I took lessons in flying pontoon planes. I invested this time, money, and attention because I found that this activity was more deeply fascinating than I had anticipated.

Why? How could an essentially technical activity, that of learning to control a machine that flies, seem absorbing to grown people? I've always enjoyed driving, especially zooming around on the open freeways of the West, but I've never spent a minute thinking about driving when I wasn't doing it, and rarely about cars unless it was time to trade mine in. I have found flying engrossing while I'm doing it, and absorbing to think about both before and after the experience.

Many of the reasons are mental and cultural: the frame of mind the activity puts me in, and the culture that surrounds the flying itself. When I first started taking lessons, one of their greatest attractions was the total concentration they demanded. The weekends in which I started going to the airport occurred during by far the most stressful part of my professional life. I had a job, that of running a magazine, with tremendous opportunities and satisfactions, but also with more than its share of nibbled-to-death-by-piranhas annoyances. It was hard not to think of these problems at 9 P.M., when I was at the office. It was hard not to think of them at 3 A.M., when I woke up wondering what the next disaster might be. But it was easy to dismiss them for the few

hours on a Saturday afternoon when every part of my consciousness would be absorbed in the struggle to understand how to *land*
the plane on the runway, rather than letting it thunk down, or
trying to figure out when to use the "carb heat" control, among a
dozen other switches in the cockpit.[1]

For people past age thirty, there is a certain time-defying satisfaction in acquiring any new skill, and that was part of this
process too. One of the many maxims of the flying world is "A
good pilot is always learning." While there may be people who
have spent so much time with this activity that everything about
it has become rote, I have sensed month by month an ever
broader range of topics that aviation makes me want to understand. For a long time, simply controlling the airplane seemed
more than enough to try to learn. After awhile, like everyone else
I learned that in good conditions—a calm day, clear skies—the
plane more or less flies itself. Or at least it does in the sense that a
bicycle more or less steers itself when you're pedaling down a
straight, flat road. Then a hundred related subjects arise. How
weather systems work. The nuances of dealing with air-traffic
controllers. How navigation systems work. How different kinds of
mountains affect the air that flows over them. What's different
about flying in the dark. What's different about flying in summer,
and in winter, and on gusty spring days. How an engine should
sound if it's running right, and what to do if it doesn't sound that
way. More about navigation. More about the weather. More and
more about weather, since it is the major variable in the safety
and comfort of a flight.

The more accustomed I became to the basic control of an airplane in flight, the more interested I became in the "multitasking"
that seems indispensable to higher levels of piloting skill. From
what I could see, the better pilots were not necessarily the ones
who could push the planes through all sorts of acrobatic maneu-

vers. Pilots who could do dives and loops and rolls were impressive, but these were not the skills I cared about. The pilots I admired were those best able to think, three steps in advance, of the many things they should be aware of and prepared for to ensure a successful flight. What radio frequencies they should be listening to, what weather reports they should be collecting, what engine functions they should be monitoring, what map or chart they needed next at hand. And all of this while keeping a careful eye on what was happening right now. I like this sort of mental juggling challenge and tried to make fewer mistakes each flight.

I enjoyed the bits of random knowledge I would never otherwise have absorbed. For instance: If you're standing in the middle of a prairie, the farthest point you can see on the horizon will be three miles away. But if you're one mile above the ground—just over 5,000 feet, a normal cruising altitude—you will be able to see 89 miles in any direction. From two miles up, 126 miles. There are formulas for these things! With my friend and pilot-aspirant Linc Caplan, I was once flying westward across Lake Michigan, from the Michigan shore toward Milwaukee. We were 10,000 feet up, nearly two miles, higher than is usually necessary in the flat Midwest, but one of the sensible precautions for a long overwater flight. (The higher you are, the farther the plane could glide to shore if it had engine problems.) The buildings of Milwaukee were twenty-five miles ahead of us. The skyscrapers of Chicago, suffused with an improbable golden light, were clearly visible seventy miles off to the left, and beyond them the steel mills of Gary at the southern end of Lake Michigan. To the right, the shore of the lake led up toward the north woods. We could take in the whole arc with a glance.

I liked learning about air-traffic routes and how to follow them. On the way to Milwaukee, we passed an imaginary point in the sky known as the "BRAVE intersection," one of the thousands of waypoints the federal air traffic control system uses to steer airplanes through the sky. The intersection names are five letters long and sometimes have a jokey relationship to the surrounding territory. In Boston there is a CELTS intersection on the south side of town. HAAVD is over Cambridge, Massachusetts, and LBSTA is just off Gloucester. Over Santa Rosa, California, where the creator of *Peanuts*, Charles Schulz, lived, there is an intersection called SNUPY. The BRAVE intersection outside Milwaukee must have been named between 1953 and 1966, the time when the Milwaukee Braves played there. Milwaukee also has SUDDS, BROTS, and GREAS.

I enjoyed the refreshing authority-inversion for adults learning to fly. Most of the people I met who were also taking lessons were men from their thirties through their fifties. While a few instructors were grizzled old coots, most were hotshots just out of college, "building time" for careers with the airlines. On a training flight down the Oregon coast, from Seattle, I went with a recent graduate of Embry-Riddle Aeronautical University who was twenty-two and looked fifteen. While we were refueling the plane in Oregon, a woman at the airport asked, "You a family?" "Teacher and student," I replied. "Is he keeping up with his homework?" she asked me. "He's the teacher," I said.

I enjoyed learning the workings of a quasi-militarized system that would be inappropriate for many activities but is highly impressive in supervising the fundamentally risky activity of flight. Pilots as a group are politically right-wing. On one check ride, when I was being inspected to see if I could handle a certain type of airplane, I performed the maneuvers while listening to the inspector give a detailed discourse about the illegitimacy of the income tax. The only proper functions of the federal government, he informed me, were the military and the airport network. If a pilot chooses his territory wisely he can find a way to fly that requires virtually no contact with the oppressive arm of the state. He can fly without speaking to air-traffic controllers, he can fly without a radio, he can fly without any electronic equipment at all, as long as he stays out of controlled airspace (and observes some other rules).

Yet with its libertarian outlook and its high premium on the prerogatives of the individual "pilot in command" of each flight, the aviation world is subject to more rigorous internal checks and balances than any other system I have experienced. Its organizing principle is that everyone is fallible and therefore everyone must undergo repeated checks. A pilot's license (or "certificate," as it's officially called) is open-ended and remains valid unless for some reason it is revoked. But everything about the right to use it is subject to constant requalifications and reexaminations. A pilot must pass a medical exam at intervals from every six months to every three years, depending on his age and whether he is carrying passengers for hire. The exams are not that thorough, but they weed out many people who would still be allowed to drive. All pilots are supposed to have a flight review every two years, unless they've gone to special refresher classes. If they want others to ride in the plane with them, they must have met certain standards in the last three months. If they want to fly at night, they must have done other things. If they want to be able to file and fly instrument-flight plans, they must have kept their instrument rating "current" by meeting other standards. Nearly every gauge, engine part, and structural element of an airplane also has its schedule for being rechecked.

And those doing the inspections are checked too. Air-traffic controllers are listening to hear how the pilots respond—but everything a controller says is captured on tape, for supervisors to review. My one run-in with aviation authority happened at Oakland Airport, when I was taxiing a plane to get ready to take off and a controller instructed me to "proceed forward from current position." I did so, and this put me right onto a runway, where another plane might have been planning to take off or land (although none were). Another controller chewed me out angrily over the radio, but I knew it would be worse for the person who had given me the wrong command, once the tapes were reviewed.

Flight instructors have godlike status with their students, but the instructors too must be checked at regular intervals by supervisors or other instructors. When I took the check ride for an instrument rating, my heart sank when I learned that I should expect not one but two passengers in the plane. One would be a normal examiner, who would sit next to me and see whether I met the standards. The other would be some supervising examiner, from the Federal Aviation Administration, who was there to see how the normal examiner was examining me. And no doubt someone would eventually be double-checking this supervisor. (At the last minute, the super-examiner cancelled, to my relief and the normal examiner's too.)

All this could sound like the old East German police state, but to me it expressed the egalitarian sensibility that everyone can make mistakes, that anyone can start coasting, that coasting and mistakes are dangerous, and that therefore we all need reminders to keep on our toes. I often think about the benefits similar systems would bring in other lines of work.

I enjoyed one final aspect of the culture of flight, which is what it taught about the difference between rationally accepted risks and pure primal fear. By the time a student pilot is ready for a first solo flight, he knows, intellectually, that the plane's nature is to fly rather than plummet to the ground. He knows that he is himself capable of bringing the plane in for a landing. By this point the student will have carried out dozens of landings with the instructor sitting next to him, providing reassurance through his presence but doing none of the actual work. Similarly, by the time the instructor lets the student go for his first solo flight, the instructor also knows that the student can land the plane safely. The percentage of mishaps on first solos is very low.

But the moment when the instructor gets out of the plane and the student sits preparing for his first unaccompanied takeoff begins a several-minute portion of life no one who has been through it ever forgets. As a student preparing for a solo, you know that once you push in the throttle and get far enough down the runway that you can't just cut the power and stop the plane, there is absolutely no way out of the situation other than accomplishing a landing by yourself. It highlights the tension between the supposedly logical left side of the brain, which knows you can do this because you have done it dozens of times with the instructor watching, and the right side, which is thinking: My God, we're going to die! The first solo flight I took is currently the most vivid of the many "firsts" in my life. No doubt that's mainly because it's the most recent, but it is also because pushing in the throttle and thinking, "Let's go," is such an act of will.

I believe that most aviation enthusiasts would give some of the same reasons for saying that they "love" to fly. But there is one other aspect I think nearly all would identify. The best name I've heard for it is "visual romance." It is the intoxication of seeing the world from above. Because it is so important a part of the enthusiast's outlook, let me try to illustrate it this way.


Before I took the trip from Oakland to Boston with my family in the small plane, I had to get the plane to Oakland. The plane was normally based in Duluth, Minnesota, at the headquarters of its manufacturer, Cirrus Design. So I took a one-way commercial flight to Minneapolis and rented a car for the three-hour drive north to Duluth. Why did I drive? Because with hub-and-spoke pricing, a ticket from San Francisco to Duluth would have cost more than twice as much as one from San Francisco to Minneapolis. In Duluth I found the plane, a demo model of the one I had agreed to buy.

The plane had a bulbous front window, almost like a helicopter's, and a body with an hourglass shape. It was widest in the cabin, where four people could sit, then tapered back to a narrow waist just before its tail. It had swooping dark-green pinstripes along its side, and its registration number, N119CD, in large letters along the side. The plane's doors opened gull-wing style, exposing the interior with its leather seats in two-tone beige.

This plane was the Cirrus SR20, which I would take to the West Coast, in one afternoon and another day of flying, and then use to take my family to the east. In Duluth I was delighted to find that I would have a traveling companion. This was Chris Baker, a pilot and flight instructor in his midtwenties. By happy coincidence, he was not merely a flight instructor; he had been my flight instructor when I was training for an instrument rating. At the time Baker had been working at a flight school in Seattle. Now he was on contract to the company that designed and built the new airplanes, and was training their owners in how to handle

The plane: N119CD.

them. He needed a ride to the West Coast; I was pleased and relieved to have someone I still thought of as the voice of authority sitting next to me for the flight.

As in the time when he'd been my instrument instructor, Baker sat in the right seat of the plane—"shotgun" in a car, the copilot's or instructor's seat in an airplane—and I sat in the pilot's seat on the left. We set off from Duluth in mid-afternoon, and for most of the next few hours, as we headed to our planned first stop in Rapid City, South Dakota, he let me fly the plane. In practice this meant making periodic small adjustments to the autopilot, responding to calls and instructions from air-traffic control, and keeping a lookout for other planes, even though hours would pass as we flew over farms and prairie without a single other craft in view. The emptiness of the sky, except on the crowded approach routes around airports, is one of the great revelations of the small-plane culture. The sight of another plane is as much an event as a glimpse of another ship on the open sea.

But near the end of the first day's journey, when we were less than an hour from Rapid City in fading light, Baker said, "My airplane." These are the words every student recognizes as the instructor's signal that he is taking command. By habit I said back, "Your airplane"; this is part of the protocol for "positive exchange of controls," to be clear about who's supposed to be in charge.[2] We were flying over the Badlands when Baker took over, roughly following the Missouri River where it seemed to be a mile wide. I'd been keeping the plane 2,000 or 3,000 feet above the ground— low enough for a much more dramatic view than is available from 35,000 feet inside an airliner, high enough not to worry that turbulence, gusts of wind, or some other surprise force would bring us unpleasantly near to earth. Baker had been patient with this— nice, prudent behavior from a low-time pilot—but with "My airplane" he proceeded to show us what the country looked like up close.

He directed us right over the center of the vast Missouri River, and then headed the plane down. This was territory Lewis and Clark had traveled. When we were not a few thousand feet over the river's surface but a few hundred, it felt as if we were re-creating their voyage. Along the banks of the river we could see stands of poplar, thickets of reeds, clouds of birds that sometimes erupted in flight as we passed by and sometimes sat unconcerned. I'd been airborne this close to the surface before—when learning to fly pontoon planes on the Puget Sound—but not at well over 150 miles an hour, nor while slaloming to follow the river's bends, nor in a place so utterly remote from any sign of human activity. To see the "flyover" zones of the American continent from an airliner is to have some theoretical awareness of how much of the landscape is unpopulated. To fly for hour upon hour at low altitude, in a little plane, and only occasionally come across an isolated ranch house or a gravel road leaves an entirely different impression. It was odd and, I'm sure, in some way dishonorable that in a modern, noisy flying machine I felt closer to nature and the wilderness than I could remember feeling when going on a hike. But the truth is that with the two of us inside that little cabin, following the river toward the setting sun with no lights or roads in view, it was like riding in a dugout canoe, a pirogue.

Eventually the sun set, and the terrain rose as we continued toward the mountains, and our destination of Rapid City neared. Baker said, "Your airplane," and I took the controls and returned to staid, normal flight as I prepared for the approach to the airport. But after landing and going to the hotel for the overnight stay, I remembered the voyage down the Missouri.

The next morning, Baker and I climbed into a van outside the Rapid City Radisson and took the brief ride back to the local airport. There were other vans and RVs on the road, many of them containing tourists on their way to visit Mount Rushmore, two dozen miles to the west. We were headed to see Mount Rushmore, too, but from a different perspective.

We loaded our bags into the plane; I started the engine; I took off and guided the plane toward the west. Then I said "Your airplane" to Baker. I said it at the moment Mount Rushmore came into view. For the next ten minutes, Baker flew the plane in among the peaks of the Black Hills, touring Mount Rushmore more or less the way it looked in the movie *North by Northwest*.

In a book of essays called *Inside the Sky*, the writer and veteran pilot William Langewiesche describes "the aerial view"—the sense of the landscape's knit-together nature that you can get neither from ground level nor by looking out the side window of an airliner but uniquely from a small plane a few thousand feet up. Langewiesche's father, Wolfgang, was a career pilot and the author of the single most influential book on the art of flying, *Stick and Rudder*, never out of print since its publication in 1944. William Langewiesche had grown up in airplanes, and he wrote that his long childhood experience with low-altitude views from his father's plane taught him to take for granted the "pilot's integrated sense of the earth's geometry":

> It wasn't until college, when I took an air-taxi job and began carrying passengers for hire, people unaccustomed to flight, that I realized that there was anything unusual about the view.... For me it was like witnessing Stone Age people seeing photographs for the first time, getting used to the scale, then turning with growing excitement from the magic to the content of the picture. These passengers had ridden on the airlines but had been herded into their cabin seats, distracted by magazines, and given shoulder-height, triple-pane windows at right

angles to the direction of flight.... And now suddenly they found themselves in a cockpit wrapped in glass, awash in brilliant light, in a small airplane lingering near the ground.[3]

The most dramatic surprise in the low-altitude aerial view is the connectedness of physical features that seem separate from the ground. The route you're on never comes to a dead end, there are no walls over which you can't look. The central city spills into the suburbs, the suburbs spill into the farmland; everything is closer and more intimate-seeming than even on a map, with its emphasis on roads and boundaries. But there are many other surprises, including the foreshortening of features that look imposing when seen from below. The physical features of a landscape have a scale best appreciated from a low-altitude plane; the human constructions usually seem overmatched. Once, with a friend, Sam Howe Verhovek, I was flying a little rented plane through the eastern hinterland of Washington State—the rangelands on the far side of the Cascade mountains from Seattle. Something too big to comprehend from the ground was unmistakable from the air: the enormous gorge that was carved tens of thousands of years earlier by the sudden emptying of "Lake Bonneville," which during the last Ice Age had covered much of the mountain Northwest. The part of this gorge that cut through the Columbia Plateau in central Washington was known as the Grand Coulee, from the French word for gorge. The lake created by the Grand Coulee dam fills up part of it. From the air, the original Coulee itself has the clarity and drama of a crater on the moon—while the man-made Grand Coulee dam, largest concrete structure ever built, seems squat and compact rather than overwhelming from above.

Something similar was true of the Black Hills and Mount Rushmore. As we came around a bend and saw the famous four carved faces, they were like scrimshaw, or Japanese netsuke. The carefully worked figures were impressive mainly for being embedded in, almost concealed by, such a vastly larger, natural background. There was a backstage quality to this look. From just above, we could see how rock debris had been unloaded in the area behind George Washington's head, giving it the appearance of a construction-zone dump—and that the backs of the heads were entirely unfinished. Baker swooped through the hills to the far-less-finished monumental statue of Crazy Horse, under construction for more than fifty years, by three generations of the Ziolkowski family of sculptors, and with many years of work still ahead. Yet if the monumental carvings seemed small, almost cute, the mountains had a coherence about them. They looked not like separated peaks but like the connected crests of waves on the sea.

Weaving through the mountains, at an altitude that gave him a comfortable margin but would have frightened me, Baker suddenly put the plane into a steep turn. It was if the plane were suspended by one wingtip, while we circled around a site on the ground pointed out by the tip of the other wing. In the middle of nowhere—a cliché that seems literally true countless times on flights in the American West—Baker had spotted a structure. It was on the top of the highest peak for miles around. At first I thought it was a house, and then I realized it was an elaborate lookout post, made of stones fitted together as in some Norman castle tower. There was no road leading to it and we could barely make out even a footpath.

Its prominence over the surrounding landscape was so great that I could not help myself. I said what anyone naturally would say on encountering such a scene. "Would you *look* at that! Can you imagine the view they must have from there?" Baker looked at me with dismay, an expression I recalled from many episodes during instrument training. He seemed to be hoping for a sign that I was being sarcastic and therefore hadn't said something as obtuse as it would seem at face value. He saw no such sign and burst out laughing—as I did half a second later. "You don't have to 'imagine' anything about it," he said when he stopped laughing. "Just look around!"

Just looking around is the heart of what has fascinated people about flying. It inspired the enthusiasts who will create a new way to travel.

# The Boys from Baraboo

Aviation companies tend to be in out-of-the-way places, for reasons that make sense as soon as you think about them. The factories need lots of space. It's no problem at all for a company that makes airplanes to fly in visitors or supplies and fly out its finished products. The aircraft workforce is partly composed of professionals—engineers and designers—many of whom seem to enjoy the life that professional salaries can buy in rural areas and small towns more than they miss the attractions of big-city life. The rest of the employees are skilled production workers—machinists, electricians, welders—whose services the company can hire at a lower prevailing wage in, say, Wichita, Kansas, than in San Francisco.

Thus Wichita is the headquarters of the Cessna Aircraft Company, which since World War II has made more "general aviation" aircraft than any other company in the world. ("General aviation" includes any airplane not operated by the military or a scheduled airline company. Of the roughly 220,000 registered airplanes in the United States, more than 90 percent are general aviation, or "GA" craft. All airlines together operate about 7,000.) The Beech division of Raytheon, which produces a renowned GA plane called the Beech Bonanza, is also based in Wichita. One of the best-known makers of instruments for small planes is the Garmin company, of Olathe, Kansas. The Mooney Aircraft Corporation, which specializes in very fast, sleek, Porsche-like private planes, is based in Kerrville, Texas, a tiny hamlet in the hill country west of San Antonio.

By the standards of its business, then, the Cirrus Design company took a conventional approach when it decided in 1993 to build a factory in Duluth, Minnesota, with its population of roughly 100,000. Before that, the company had operated out of a barn in Baraboo, Wisconsin, population 10,000. The main alternative it had considered before moving to Duluth was Grand Forks, North Dakota.

Certain sections of today's Duluth are as bedraggled as any other old-economy remnant. The main businesses that sustained the city before World War II—shipping flour, processing and shipping iron ore—have been in decline for decades. But the waterfront area, on the southwestern tip of Lake Superior, has undergone an expensive and successful renovation. Through the summer its luxurious hotels and bars are crowded with tourists headed for the nearby Apostle Islands. In the winter, it is more crowded, with snowmobilers and cross-country skiers, and when hunting season opens in the fall it is most crowded of all. In addition to tourism, the city has recovered by developing medical centers and colleges. And it hopes it will soon be the "next Wichita," the next center of business success in aviation.

The vessel of these hopes is a stark, white, large warehouse-sized building on the north end of town, with the word "Cirrus" in black sans-serif letters along the top edge.

The building adjoins the two-mile-long runway at Duluth International Airport. This runway, nearly the size of the main ones at LAX or JFK, was built when the airport was a cold war air force base, supporting fighters on alert to head north. When the base was closed in the early nineties, its main buildings became a federal minimum-security prison. In 1994, Cirrus Design moved onto nearby land to begin its operations.

Cirrus was incorporated in the early eighties by two brothers, Alan and Dale Klapmeier, both then in their twenties. They had grown up in Illinois and Wisconsin in a family of tinkerers and business-starters. One uncle had founded and become successful with a company that manufactured fiberglass pleasure boats. In the mid-sixties, when both boys were in grade school, their parents founded a chain of three nursing homes, which became successful and profitable. The boys took summer jobs at the nursing homes to earn their spending money. The Klapmeiers' homes offered an upscale, resortlike atmosphere. In one, there was a fountain in the main reception hall and a large atrium. In 1984 a

The Cirrus Design factory in Duluth, summer 2000.

hospital chain bought the three homes for about $15 million. What the parents wanted the children to think was not "Now we are rich!" but instead "Now we have working capital."

"We came from a family where even as kids, it was not seen as unrealistic to be thinking about starting your own company, being good at developing it," Alan Klapmeier told me when I first met him, in 1999. "But one of the things we learned from our parents was that running your own business wasn't some eight-to-five situation. We'd always be going over there on the weekend or late at night. I remember one time my dad asking, Is there anything you think we ought to be doing differently? I was a third grade kid, so I said, Well, I think it needs a flagpole outside. And they thought it was a good idea! We got used to the idea that there'd be an atmosphere of group discussion in the family and everyone adding their ideas."

From the time they were little, Alan and Dale Klapmeier assumed that when they started a company of their own, it would have something to do with airplanes. Alan Klapmeier says, "I can't remember a time when I wasn't interested in airplanes." His mother later told him that until the age of two the only times he'd stop crying were when she'd drop whatever else she was doing and turn her full attention to him—or when she would drive to a viewing area near the O'Hare Airport approach path and put him in a bassinet on the hood of the car, where he could watch the planes.

Alan has become a stocky, square-faced grownup with bushy light hair. He loves explaining his ideas and talking over all the reasons why his company is destined to succeed. As is the case with many entrepreneurs, he is an extrovert. It is easy to believe that as a baby he would have cried whenever his mother looked away. It seems natural that Alan Klapmeier has been Mr. Outside for the company since the start—talking to investors, reporters, and potential customers. His brother Dale, three years younger, is taller, lankier, and more taciturn—a man who likes fast airplanes, automobiles, and motorcycles. When I saw him one day at the factory wearing a black leather jacket and heavy boots, I felt I had glimpsed him in his natural state. Dale has been Mr. Inside, concentrating on how the products are conceived, designed, and built. Paul Johnston, an engineer who dropped out of graduate school to join the company in 1989, says that Alan Klapmeier's distinctive strength is "doing the part of the job I personally understand least: going out and generating the interest, getting the money, and making sure Dale has the resources to get planes designed and out the door." Dale's part of the job has been to "really make sure that things on the physical side happen at a very good rate," and that the company does what it says. There is a third Klapmeier brother, the eldest, Ernie, who has a small business of his own but has not been directly involved in Cirrus.

When Alan Klapmeier got glasses at age nine, he gave up his dream of being an air force pilot. But he still wrote school book reports on aviation, built model planes with Dale, and discussed flying with their uncle the boat builder, who owned a floatplane. By his sophomore year in high school he had talked his parents into letting him start flying lessons. His parents went with him to "ground school"—the classes in navigation and weather and engine maintenance that prospective pilots take in preparation for written FAA exams—to get an idea of how dangerous this really was. His father got a license, and then agreed that Alan could start work on his. His mother became a pilot too. Alan used his earnings from summer work at the nursing home to pay for his flight training, and soon after graduating from high school he became a licensed pilot.

After Alan went off to Ripon College, a few hours away by car, he began hinting that he'd come home more often if he could do it by air. By this time his parents had bought the family's first plane, a 1960 model Cessna 182, which they used for family trips and for his father's business travel. "Dad never actually liked to fly," Alan says. "But he saw the practical benefits of getting around for business. He stopped flying once he sold the company and bought a motor home instead." When Alan was in college, the three Klapmeier brothers shared the cost of a thirty-year-old Cessna 140, a single-engine, high-wing, tail-wheel model regarded as a timeless classic. The brothers bought the plane more or less in the way other young men might buy a classic T-bird or Mustang and then lovingly restore it. The total cost of the plane was $5,200. When split three ways, this was less than the cost of a typical car of the time. Dale, who was still in high school, took his flying lessons in the plane. He therefore was known in high school as the only student who could fly the family plane before he drove the family car.

When Dale graduated from high school in 1979, he, Alan, and Alan's college roommate, Jeff Viken, bought a junked plane, a 1960 Champ, and spent the summer rebuilding it. Then Dale went off to the University of Wisconsin–Stevens Point to study business and economics. Alan had studied physics and economics at Ripon, and worked in the Ripon admissions office while Dale finished college. Meanwhile the brothers kept talking about when they'd start their airplane company and what kind of planes they would sell.

"The only way Alan and I could afford to fly on our own was to buy wrecked planes and fix them up," Dale told me in our first meeting. "Then we bought a Glasair kit plane when I was a soph-omore in college. The people who designed *that* plane were just out of college themselves. They thought they had a better idea and wanted to try it. We thought we could do it too.

"And Alan always had this airplane design in his head as a dream. That is when we started talking about, Let's go do this. We can do it, we can build an airplane. I guess I never had a real job, because when I graduated from college, we just went straight into designing and building our own airplane.

"We weren't raised with the idea that you go to college and then go get a job someplace. The whole family has been entrepreneurs. The attitude we were raised with was, You can go do it. Take your destiny in your own hands."

The world into which the brothers made this plunge is hard for most people in the twenty-first century to envision, because of a peculiarity of culture and a major shift of economic circumstance. The culture that the Klapmeiers first entered was that of the "kit plane" builder, a kind of enthusiast elite among the enthusiasts. The most obvious advantage that kit planes have over "certified" airplanes, those that the Federal Aviation Administration has tested extensively and approved as safe for general sale, is price. In the seventies, certified airplanes like the Cessna 172 or Grumman Tiger cost $25,000 and up, and the fancy models like the Beech Bonanza started at $80,000. Comparable kit planes cost about a third as much. In the 2000s, virtually the only way to get a new plane for less than $100,000 is to buy a kit. The typical kit requires many hundreds of hours of skilled work for assembly, but if someone has more skill and time than money it can be a worthwhile trade-off.

But for the enthusiasts whose culture revolves around kit planes, cost is not the only advantage of building their own craft, nor even the most important one. The idea of living free of the regulating hand of the state is what really seems to excite them. Unless a plane has been through the arduous, years-long testing process for FAA certification, it must at all times carry prominent placards over its doors and on its instrument panel saying "Exper-

imental." Every time its pilots talk over the radio, they must identify themselves as flying an "Experimental" craft. ("Los Angeles
Center, this is Experimental Five-Niner-Three, inbound for landing ...") Behind these rules is a "watch out, Buster" attitude from
the FAA: regulatory officialdom is taking no responsibility what-
soever for the soundness or safety of these craft, and people getting in them are assuming all the risks.

The reality behind this attitude is that experimental craft genuinely are several times more dangerous even than other small
airplanes.[1] The culture of small planes in general involves deliberately accepted risk, a crucial theme to which we'll return. But
with kit planes nearly all the risk is accepted by the builder and
pilot, usually the same person, since the normally hyperattentive
safety inspectors from the government wash their hands of
responsibility for the craft altogether.

That is, you might say, the downside. But it is striking how
much *less* frequently discussions of safety and accident-prevention
crop up at kit plane conventions or in their publications than in
those designed for the pilots of mainstream, government-certified
planes. What kit plane enthusiasts talk about is the flexibility and
freedom they have to dream up, design, build, and fly new kinds
of aerial machines. The Experimental Aircraft Association's Summer AirVenture convention in Oshkosh, is the main showcase for
people who want to introduce whole new concepts for planes.
Planes that look like flying saucers; planes with swooping futuristic lines; "canard"-style planes, with small wings in the front of
the plane and larger ones in back that made the plane look as if it
were flying in reverse. (Canard means "duck" in French, and the
planes picked up this nickname because with so much of their
body in front of the wings they looked like ducks in flight.) The
Voyager experimental airplane, which in 1986 set a long-range
flight record by flying around the world nonstop, in nine days, on

a single load of fuel, was a product of the experimental/kit plane culture. Its designer, Burt Rutan, has been for years a star at the Oshkosh summer gatherings, and the Oshkosh museum has a full-scale facsimile of the plane with extensive demos about its pilots, Dick Rutan and Jeana Yeager.

The pride of the experimental aviators is that they have been the source of new ideas in an increasingly staid business. People just out of college cannot reasonably set out to build a new certified airplane, any more than they can set out to develop and quickly market a new prescription drug. Preparing enough prototypes and accumulating enough test data to satisfy federal safety standards takes tens of millions of dollars and at least several years. But youngsters and newcomers can realistically plan to dream up an airplane, build and test-fly it on their own, and then work the kit plane–show circuit in hopes of getting others to buy. "Our dream had always been to have a company building certified airplanes," Dale Klapmeier says. "But at the time we started, the whole industry seemed to be going down the toilet, so to even think that we could raise the money for certified production aircraft, it was basically absurd. But the experimental avenue was a way to get into aviation."

That was the route they took. As soon as Dale finished college in 1984, he and Alan began working together. By 1986 they had incorporated Cirrus Design. With Jeff Viken, the roommate of Alan's who had majored in physics and math at Ripon College, they worked round the clock in the barn in Baraboo to design a spaceship-looking craft they called the VK-30. The initials in its name were for Viken and Klapmeier, and the look of the VK-30 expresses the kit plane world's impatience with the stodginess of Cessna/Piper style design.

The plane looked unusual, because its propeller was at the rear, "pusher" style, rather than in the front. It had a relatively fat

**The Cirrus VK-30 in flight.**

though streamlined body, as in a child's drawing of a spaceship, and it was driven by an engine that could take it to nearly 300 miles per hour.[2] It was designed to hold five passengers.

Like many other experimental planes, the VK-30 was built of composite material, mainly fiberglass, rather than the bent-and-pounded aluminum panels of most GA planes. The advantage of composite construction was that the plane's contours could easily be curved and swooshed in any way the designers chose. Metal airplanes, by contrast, are an assemblage of panels and rolled pieces that are connected with rivets. The sleeker, suppler curves of a composite design meant that a plane could be more "slippery" as it moved through the air, generating less aerodynamic drag, and this in turn meant that it might go farther and faster on a given amount of power and fuel. The start-up costs for a factory building composite planes were also relatively low, since the molds and forms necessary to shape the fiberglass parts were cheap compared with most metal-working equipment.

In addition, composite manufacturing techniques allow an airplane to be made of a small number of large pieces—two halves of a fuselage, for instance, or a wing consisting of one top section and one bottom section, joined around a spar—rather than hundreds of metal pieces fitted and riveted together. This can make the planes stronger, far easier to manufacture, and all the smoother in the air because of the absence of protruding seams or connectors. The main drawback of composites is that they are heavier than aluminum, for comparable levels of strength, and often more expensive. The trick with composites is working the trade-offs so that the aerodynamic advantages offset the penalty of weight.

The VK-30 did not make its first flight until early 1988, but the Klapmeiers and Viken displayed a prototype, to wide acclaim, at the Oshkosh summer air show in 1987. The plane turned out to be a succès d'estime as well as a "success d'engineering." It drew crowds at Oshkosh. It appeared on the cover of thirteen aviation-related magazines and was the first kit plane ever to be on the cover of the influential publication *Aviation Week and Space Technology*. It established the young Klapmeiers, Viken, and Cirrus as forces to watch in the world of airplane design. But it didn't sell.

"We wanted to make this an extremely capable airplane," Dale Klapmeier says. "So it was expensive and hard to build. We were looking for people with a couple hundred thousand dollars to spend on it, and the skill and time to put years of work into it. Those people are not out there."

The Klapmeiers were discouraged but not beaten by the VK-30's market difficulties. They tried to sort out the lessons the plane had taught them about technology, about financing, and about demand in the marketplace. From what they'd heard from potential customers, most of whom finally decided not to buy the VK-30, they believed the best market opportunities were for two quite different products. One would be a small, safe, relatively inexpensive "entry level" plane, with a piston-driven engine and fixed landing gear, which would hold four passengers and compete with the existing, aging Cessnas and Pipers. The other would be a plane roughly similar to the VK-30. That is, a very fast, relatively costly five-passenger plane with a shape like the VK-30's and a turboprop engine in the rear.

Which way should they go? It would depend on which idea could attract investment capital first. "Lots of people would call and tell us, 'That VK-30 was great, let's try to build a certified model!'" Alan Klapmeier says. "And then we'd start talking about all the necessary changes, and it would never get anywhere. So we boiled it down to a simple statement. If someone said they were interested in a certified model, we'd say: If you're really interested, come visit us." Finally a group of financiers from Switzerland flew to Wisconsin to meet the Klapmeiers. The Swiss thought there were strong commercial prospects for a high-end, turboprop model. So the Cirrus Design Corporation's first attempt at building a certified airplane would be a turboprop.

The new plane would be named the ST50. The name was based on a scheme of nomenclature the Klapmeiers had worked out when dreaming of the time when Cirrus would offer a full product line of a dozen or more planes, from inexpensive "starter" models to personal jets. The "S" was for single-engine, in contrast to twin-engine planes like the Beech Baron. "T" was for turbine power. The number 50 gave an idea of where the plane would fit in the ultimate, and at the time theoretical, product line. The "50 series" would be very fast, very expensive planes. The ST50, designed to travel at well over 300 miles per hour, would be priced at $1 million, and might be followed by an ST52 and ST54 model. (The company stopped using a hyphen in the model name after the VK-30.) The "20" series would be the least expensive airplanes. The simpler plane the Klapmeiers were considering at the same time would be known as the SR20—a single-engine, four-passenger, reciprocating (piston-powered) plane that they thought would cruise at 180 miles an hour and cost under $150,000.

Like the VK-30 kit model, the ST50 encountered market difficulties. The project had started very promisingly. In 1992, Cirrus signed a $13 million contract with Israviation, a government-sponsored aircraft start-up company in Israel. Israviation promised to pay the money for a working, tested, performing-to-spec prototype of the plane. Cirrus would then turn the prototype and all specifications, drawings, and plans over to Israviation, which would manufacture the ST50 in Israel. Cirrus would have the rights to sell the plane in North America, for a flat 10 percent commission on the planned $1 million price.

The ST50 prototype made its first, fully successful test flight on December 7, 1994, and Cirrus delivered it to Israviation the following May. In a business plan the Klapmeiers prepared soon

The Cirrus ST50.

after this delivery, they envisioned raising $10 million in working capital for the first stage of their company's progress toward developing and building a larger product line, and estimated that they would sell the first three ST50s in 1996, then fifty in 1998, then one hundred in 2000.

In fact, they did not deliver any. Israviation proved to operate on political-economic rather than normal economic principles. The Israeli government planned to back Israviation as a way of building the nation's technology base and creating high-skill jobs in northern Israel. Under the funding model, Israviation would invest money first and would eventually be reimbursed by the government. The reimbursement came too slowly, political arguments engulfed the program, and Israviation went out of business before completing a production or marketing system. In the end only two working models of the ST50 were built.

The deal was another defeat, typical of the experience of most aircraft start-ups, but it helped keep Cirrus going. The company had gained steadily more experience with composite manufacturing. The cash flow from the Israviation contract, plus other small projects and prototypes they did for other manufacturers, allowed them to meet the payroll month by month.

Through the late eighties, when the brothers were entering their thirties, they lived on their family's farm, worked in Baraboo in new buildings they'd erected at the local airport, got fiberglass at a discount through their uncle's boat works. The engine for the first VK-30 prototype came out of a junkyard. From the Klapmeier family's point of view, the business was becoming a more and more serious investment. The senior Klapmeiers had put nearly three and a half million dollars into their sons' company by this point.

Yet by the standards of the airplane business, Cirrus was operating on a shoestring. "Where'd we get 'all the money' to build the company?" Dale Klapmeier asks rhetorically. "We didn't use a lot of money. All through our history it's been, How do we do something and spend as little money as possible doing it?"

The guerrilla approach cost the Klapmeiers the partnership of Jeff Viken, who was offered a more secure job as a NASA contractor and, after some agonizing, took it. But other young engineers, drawn by the publicity for the VK-30, drove to the barn in Baraboo and asked if they could join Cirrus. One was Pat Waddick, who had just finished his course in engineering at the University of Wisconsin. In the summer of 1989 he drove to Baraboo and asked for a job. Alan Klapmeier said the company wasn't hiring. "I'll do anything," Waddick said. "Will you sweep the floors?" Klapmeier asked. "Yes." Klapmeier told him to take up a broom and get to work. "He just wouldn't take No for an answer," Klapmeier now says. By the mid-nineties Waddick had become the company's vice president in charge of engineering.

Paul Johnston also arrived in 1989. Alan Klapmeier had met Johnston the previous year, as Johnston was beginning graduate school at the University of Minnesota. Johnston had gone to Ames, Iowa, for the summer to work on a Glasair kit plane. Alan Klapmeier had gone to Ames to display a Glasair plane that he and Dale had built. He took Johnston up for a short ride, which became a long ride as Klapmeier described the plans for the VK-30. The two stayed in touch, and after Johnston had begun work for a master's degree at the University of Minnesota, Klapmeier flew up to meet him and told him that he had to quit his studies and join the company. After deliberating over the Christmas holidays, Johnston agreed to drop out of graduate school and sign on with Cirrus. He is now the company's chief engineer.

"What amazed me was their follow-through," Johnston says. "People would always come up at air shows and say, We're working on a new design, doing this or that. You'd never hear of it again. I met Alan, he told me about this VK-30 project, how they were going to design and fly it. I thought: Yeah, sure, good luck. Then I showed up at Oshkosh next year, and there was the proto-type! When they asked me to come aboard, I thought: These guys said it, and it happened."

Waddick and Johnston, both in their thirties and both centrally responsible for the design and evolution of Cirrus airplanes, are an oddly matched, occasionally quarrelsome, but usefully comple-mentary pair. Johnston, with a thick mop of dark hair, is intense, sarcastic, wisecracking, and absent-minded. He is also regarded as the most naturally gifted engineer in the organization. He would be a familiar figure in any software company or Internet start-up, where the halls are full of software developers whose technical brilliance excuses a lot of oddball personal traits. Pat Waddick is careful, methodical, less eloquent, less flashy, more neatly groomed, but adept in making sure that the right mix of talents is applied in the right way. The two of them mirror the dispositions and talents of the Klapmeier brothers—Alan voluble, flashy, free-wheeling; Dale methodical and organized. "What I hope I have in creativity, and what Dale has in mechanical instincts, and what Paul has in real brilliance when it comes to looking at numbers, Pat has in organizational ability," Alan Klapmeier says. "It doesn't matter how good your idea is, if you can't do it all by yourself you've got to organize others to do it. That is Pat's skill."

The Cirrus team in Baraboo was young, enthusiastic, whole-somely Midwestern, appropriately cocky. Yet the objective reali-ties of the airplane business could hardly be encouraging to them. The VK-30 kit plane had failed. The ST50 was failing. As if that were not enough, they faced a fundamental obstacle. Dale Klap-meier had been right when he said that the small-aircraft business as a whole was "going down the toilet."

For reasons that are still debated today, in a surprisingly short time, from the late seventies through the mid-eighties, the market for small airplanes almost disappeared, and small-plane flying became an even less mainstream activity than it had previously been.

At the end of World War II, the United States had a large supply of recently trained pilots and a huge aircraft-manufacturing base. At the peak of wartime production, in 1944, American factories had produced some 100,000 military planes. Just after the war, in 1946, about 35,000 small general aviation planes were made and sold.[3] The annual shipments fell sharply through the postwar period, but as the wartime generation—the baby boomers' parents—prospered and matured in the fifties and sixties, the small-plane business grew with them. Through the fifties, small-plane sales averaged about 6,000 a year. Through the sixties, they averaged more than 10,000. Through the seventies they boomed: more than 14,000 in 1974, more than 15,000 in 1976, nearly 18,000 in 1978. The population of active pilots grew at the same time, to more than 825,000 in 1980.

Suddenly it all collapsed. By 1981, airplane shipments were 9,000, only half as high as three years earlier. In 1982, they had fallen by more than half again, to 4,200. In 1983, they again fell nearly by half, to 2,600. By the early nineties the small-plane factories were turning out barely 1,000 planes a year, and the population of active pilots was falling toward a low of around 600,000 in 1997. In the mid-seventies, 200,000 students a year had begun flying lessons. In the early nineties, half as many did. The Piper Aircraft Corporation, creator of the famous Cub, went into bankruptcy. (It has since reemerged, as New Piper Aircraft.) In 1986, soon after Cirrus incorporated, Cessna suspended its production of small propeller planes.

The companies had various explanations for what had happened. Perhaps it was the historic rise in oil prices that OPEC began in the early seventies, which made flying more expensive. Or perhaps not—the peak in small-plane sales came six years after the first oil shock. Perhaps it was that times were bad in the early eighties and people had too little extra income. Or perhaps not, since the plunge continued through better economic times later in the eighties. Perhaps it was that very rebound in the eighties: as people became richer, they had an ever-wider variety of choices for their leisure time. Perhaps it was the elimination of an artificial incentive to buy airplanes. Until the tax reforms of the eighties, small airplanes had generally been eligible for the federal "investment tax credit," which offset a significant share of their cost. Perhaps the phenomenon was mainly demographic. The market for airplanes boomed during the sixties and early seventies, when the large cohort of pilots trained by the military for World War II and the Korean War came of age and prospered, and it declined as that generation aged.

Perhaps it was all these factors, which together depressed the market in a way no one of them could have in isolation. But most of all, in the view of the small-plane establishment, the problem was the lawyers. Every time there was a plane crash, there was likely to be a follow-up liability suit against the manufacturers. A pilot may have taken off without making sure he had enough gas— and then crashed a few minutes later when the engine stopped. Juries increasingly found manufacturers liable for negligence in such cases, and awarded ever-escalating compensation. From the manufacturers' point of view, the worst aspect of the liability law was that it had no end point or statute of limitations. They could be sued for accidents in planes they had built twenty, thirty, or forty years earlier, which meant that each new plane they built added to their total exposure. Much as happened with medical malpractice fees, liability insurance fees rose dramatically within a decade. The president of Cessna contended in 1985, as his company was leaving the small-plane business, that liability insurance costs represented 20 to 30 percent of the cost of each new plane.

Led by Cessna, and backed by Democratic and Republican members alike from Kansas's delegation in Congress, small-air-plane companies claimed more and more insistently through the early nineties that they would go out of business altogether unless the liability rules were changed. Russ Meyer, Cessna chairman, told a congressional hearing in 1994 that his industry had "been essentially destroyed by the unlimited cost of product liability"— but promised that Cessna would reopen its small-plane factories if the GARA, the "General Aviation Revitalization Act," were passed. The Clinton administration backed GARA, which put an eighteen-year statute of limitations on liability claims against air-craft makers, and it became law late in 1994. The timing was con-venient for Cessna, Piper, and Beech, since they had produced very few planes in at least the previous fifteen years.

Alan and Dale Klapmeier entered the small-plane market in the downswing part of this cycle, in the late eighties. But they were convinced that lawyers and the liability laws, while a prob-lem, were not the fundamental issue. The principal reason people stopped buying airplanes, they believed, was that the planes themselves, and the whole experience of small-plane travel, were no longer worth the money. All the innovation in the flying busi-ness—improvements in comfort, price, performance, efficiency— was happening at the top of the pyramid, for the airliners and the multi-million-dollar corporate jets. Smaller planes got more expensive each year but didn't get any faster, more efficient, or more comfortable. The result was to make the aviation market like the U.S. automobile market of the seventies, before the arrival of the Japanese: tired, unexciting, overpriced. To make themselves the Japanese of the business was the Klapmeiers' goal.

"The tort issue was largely a myth," Alan Klapmeier said the first time I met him, in 1999. It was a warm day in September, and we met in his office at the Cirrus plant, with a view of the huge Duluth runway. Every ten or fifteen minutes, a pair of F-16 fighter jets from the Air National Guard station would roar down the runway and drown out our conversation. Once during the hour we talked, a new Cirrus SR20 rolled onto the runway and took off. The very first plane had been delivered to a customer only six weeks before, and at that point the Cirrus fleet consisted of fewer than half a dozen planes. We stopped talking so he could watch it through the whole several-minute process of warm-up, taxiing, and departure. Then he returned to his theme.

"The basic problem in the late seventies and eighties was that the companies stopped improving the products, so they didn't offer enough value to make it worth customers' buying them." Year after year, the manufacturers offered the same planes—the Cessna 172, the Piper Archer or Warrior, the Beech Bonanza, each essentially the same as the year before, only more expensive. "Somewhere in the late seventies, you got to a situation where you could buy a new airplane for *x* dollars, or you could buy a two-year-old version, with two hundred flying hours, for one-half *x*. The lack of product improvement simply added up to bad value." A midlevel single-engine plane cost approximately $75,000 new in 1975. Twenty years later, an almost identical plane, with some more advanced navigation systems but no faster or more efficient, could cost four times that much. "The airplanes we're competing against are Sputnik-era planes," Klapmeier says. "If you think of that little aluminum ball with wires sticking out, compared with what we have today in space, it drives home the point that these are *really old* airplanes."

Another way to demonstrate this stagnation is to flip through aviation magazines from a quarter century ago and look at the ads. The planes being shown are the same ones on sale now, but for about one-fifth the current price. A more vivid reminder is to see any movie from the sixties or seventies that includes shots of small aircraft—for instance, *It's a Mad, Mad, Mad, Mad World*, from 1963, or the original Steve McQueen–Faye Dunaway version of *The Thomas Crown Affair*, from 1968. Most of the physical details of life preserved in such films seem startlingly different from those of the early 2000s, as if we were already looking at museum-worthy material. The phones with rotary dials, the total absence of cell phones, the big vinyl records on hi-fi sets, the chunky, clunky cars, apart from the original Mustang.

Everything is different—except the airplanes, which look completely up-to-date, because they are identical to the ones you would find at a small airport today. The twin-engine Beech Baron and single-engine Bonanza. The high-wing Cessna 172 and 182. The Piper Warriors and Cherokees. Not only are the designs unchanged over the decades; unless they have crashed in the meantime, the very planes shown in those films are likely still to be in service now. My two sons were born in 1977 and 1980. Every plane I have rented in the years between starting flying lessons and getting my own plane was older than my boys. "In the late sixties, there was a tremendous debate as to whether we should continue to allow World War II aircraft to fly as they were over 20 years old, a shocking age at the time," the aviation columnist Rick Durden wrote in December 2000. "Now, if you can find a good, used airplane that is less than 20 years old, at a decent price, it is unusual."[4]

And the underlying designs and technology of these airplanes are much older than the actual crafts. The most popular small GA planes, the high-wing Cessna 172 Skyhawk and 182 Skylane, are basically unchanged from the models first introduced in the early fifties. In 1997 the Beech Bonanza celebrated its fiftieth anniversary in more or less continuous production. Of course there have been changes over the years, mainly in instrumentation. But to see one of these planes is to have no doubt that it is an ambassador from a much earlier age.

It is possible to view such a venerable fleet as a sign that these were products built to last. This was the spin that an executive of the New Piper Aircraft company put on the situation in the nineties: "Our airplanes are well designed and well built, often remaining in service for thirty years or longer." But almost any product—a car, a refrigerator, a 1981 original IBM Personal Computer—could also be kept going for decades, just like an airplane, if like airplanes it were subject to the federal requirement for top-to-bottom annual inspections, renovations, and repairs. The only parts of the world where people actually try to keep cars going for decades, except when consciously preserving museum pieces, are places like modern Havana, where there's no incoming supply. The reason it's not done elsewhere is that new products are better. With enough effort, you could keep that 1977 Gremlin running— but you wouldn't, since the new models look better, are safer, run more efficiently, have new features, and are easier to maintain.

There were lots of reasons, including tort liability, why the small-plane fleet became stagnant, which in turn led to the collapse in sales. One was the long FAA certification process, which would have made it difficult for companies to unveil upgrades and new models every year, as automakers had done, even if the companies had wanted to. Another reason was simple complacency. "I remember some article in 1978 describing the Skyhawk as 'perhaps the perfect plane,'" Alan Klapmeier says. "I remember thinking: the Model T, 'perhaps the perfect car.'"

But the fundamental force behind the abandonment of small planes was that the companies in the airplane business directed their engineering, their investment, and their marketing higher up the value chain, toward the corporate jets they could sell to fewer customers but at a much higher margin per plane. Cessna's showcase item became the Citation business jet, the current model of which holds up to eight passengers and costs up to $12 million. Selling just one jet made more profit for the company than selling dozens of planes. The Citation showed that companies like Cessna still had plenty of creativity: this became the first nonmilitary jet that was certified for operation by a single pilot, because Cessna had put tremendous effort into making the controls as simple and streamlined as possible. The company could push advanced technology too: the latest model of the Citation can go faster than any commercial airliner except the supersonic Concorde. Compared with the previous market leader for private jets, Learjet, the Citation was seen as offering good value, and Cessna sold them by the thousands. So as Cessna, which had made more GA propeller planes than any other company, moved out of that market altogether in the mid-eighties, it had tort liability as the public excuse for what was more basically a shift in business judgment. "Pilots, with their ego, couldn't believe that no one was paying attention to them and their single-engine planes," Alan Klapmeier says. "So it was easier to tell them, We didn't want to abandon you, but those nasty tort laws just made it impossible for us."

The immediate consequence of the shift toward corporate jets was to convert the liability issue from a debating point to a genuine problem. An aircraft company's liability rates were based on the size of the fleet in service—tens of thousands of active Cessnas, several thousand Bonanzas, and so on. The fleet size didn't change much year by year. But the company had to amortize the cost of liability insurance for the existing fleet with supplements to the cost of the new planes it sold each year. When Cessna was selling 5,000 planes per year, a $10 million annual insurance bill for the existing fleet added $2,000 to the cost of each new plane.

When it was selling only 500, suddenly the per-plane insurance burden was $20,000. So whether or not insurance fees really began the decline in sales, once that decline began, the insurance problem quickly became dire. The per-plane cost of insurance went up; as new planes became more expensive, fewer of them were sold; the insurance burden got even worse; and companies just left the business.

The longer-term consequence was thoroughgoing stagnation in the design, production, marketing, and sales of small planes. Engineers were still thinking of better, more efficient, and more comfortable ways to fly, and entrepreneurs were thinking of ways to satisfy new markets. But the technology, innovation, finance, and marketing efforts were all shunted away from any device for air travel other than the corporate or airline jet. If you ran an airline, you knew that major companies would be competing to provide the machines you needed. If you were a Fortune 500 corporation or a person who could imagine spending $10 million on a plane, you knew that Gulfstream, Lear, Cessna, and other companies would keep bringing out new models for your consideration. But if you were considering small-plane air travel as an alternative to the highway system or to the airlines, you had an aging, unmodernized, increasingly run-down set of equipment to deal with. It is as if people considering rental cars had only the '57 Chevies of Havana to choose from.

Apart from its impact on fleet safety, the material slowdown naturally affected public interest in the planes and in aviation in general. "Just when the industry was slowing down, everything else was speeding up," says NASA official Bruce Holmes. "In the eighties you started to have home computers. Much better cars. New kinds of wind surfers. Skis. Whole lists of things that didn't exist in the sixties. So the availability of resources for either buying or investing in planes went other places that were more interesting and changing faster."

By the time the Klapmeiers were going into business, the small-plane economy was deteriorating to such a degree that to get involved with it you had to be an enthusiast, interested in airplanes for their own sake, not as tools for getting from place to place. Most people learn to fly in the Cessna 152, a very light plane with so small a cockpit that the instructor usually has to put his arm behind the student's back when they're sitting side by side, or in the Cessna 172 Skyhawk, a larger version of the same design. They are the very opposite of stylish or graceful, but they are stable, controllable, forgiving of the many sins of the student pilot. By the time an aspiring pilot has gone through the emotional process of learning to land the plane, flying it solo the first time, and passing the "practical test," or check ride, for a private pilot's certificate, it's almost inevitable that he will view the battered 152 or Skyhawk as a trusty steed, which has borne its rider past many difficulties.

The shock comes when a civilian who has not been through this process—often the pilot's spouse, which, since most pilots are men, usually means his wife—comes along for a ride, and visibly recoils at the down-market appearance of the machine the pilot regards with such pride.

Since the early nineties cars in the United States have become pleasant to sit in—comfortable seats, modern instruments and sound systems, continually improved fit-and-finish inside. A passenger alights from such a car and looks toward a plane built in the seventies on a design from the fifties, a plane with cracked Naugahyde seats, often covered with tattered sheepskins, and a discolored plastic windshield. The passenger thinks: I'll do this once, out of love.

Thinking about it more systematically, the Klapmeiers reasoned in the early nineties that there were four things wrong with small planes that had ruined them as a business and made them ineffective as a transportation tool.

The planes were *too slow*. The Skyhawk cruised at between 100 and 120 knots, or the equivalent of 115 to 138 miles an hour.[5] When they were introduced in the fifties, that was about three times as fast as average long-distance driving speed, since the interstate highway system had not yet been built. By the nineties it was not even twice the speed of highway driving. To be attractive and efficient to anyone other than enthusiasts, the brothers reasoned, new planes would again have to become at least three times as fast as cars, which meant 180 to 200 miles an hour.

Next, the planes were *too expensive*. In the fifties, a family considering an airplane that went three times as fast as highway traffic would have to pay about four times as much as for a top-of-the-line car. In the nineties, the same plane had a smaller speed advantage over modern cars but had a larger cost penalty. A Mercedes, Lexus, Porsche, or Lincoln could cost $50,000 in the midnineties. In those same years, a new Bonanza or Mooney airplane cost between seven and ten times that much.

The existing fleet of small airplanes, even the new ones, was also *too primitive and unattractive*. The styling revolution that had touched cars, electronic equipment, kitchen and bathroom features, and other aspects of American life since the early eighties had passed small airplanes by. Comforts as widely accepted as a good music system or as trivial but appealing as cup holders were hard to obtain.

Finally, small planes were *too dangerous*, and seemed even riskier than they actually were. Many members of the nonpilot public would of course put this first on the list of reasons to avoid general aviation, for both rational and extrarational reasons. For several fundamental reasons small planes are more hazardous than big commercial ones. Small planes are more likely to rely on piston engines, which have a far greater likelihood of failure than jet engines do. An engine failure is not necessarily a catastrophe— a standard part of basic pilot training is learning to glide the plane down to a safe landing with the power off. But if it happens at night, or over water, or in the mountains it can be disastrous, and obviously engines that fail less frequently are safer. Also, small planes cannot fly as high as big airliners, and therefore they must fly around or through the clouds and storms that account for most small-plane crashes. Airliners can simply fly above nearly any weather problem except thunderstorms. The instruments in small planes are less elaborate than the costly flight decks in a jetliner, so they carry a greater risk of the pilot's getting disoriented or lost. And the pilots in small planes are on the whole less skilled, experienced, and sharp than those in the big planes—and usually they operate on their own, rather than in teams of two or three.

The extrarational force in fears about small planes comes from the impression, via news reports, that they're constantly running into each other or falling out of the sky, plus the striking number of prominent people who have died in plane crashes, especially in the fifties and sixties. General aviation accident rates have fallen by about 80 percent since the fifties, mainly because engines have become more reliable and systems for navigating through clouds have improved. On average, small planes fly a total of 70,000 to 100,000 hours each day. The figures are imprecise, because they are estimated from fuel sales and other indirect measurements. No one keeps exact count. On average, one person dies in a small plane crash each day. This is much more hazardous than the airlines and, depending on how the rate is calculated, between two and six times riskier than driving a car. For instance: a typical GA pilot might fly an average of 100 hours a year. So if the crude statistical fatality rate were one per 100,000 hours, then the typical small-plane pilot would have a one in a thousand risk of a fatal crash per year.

People who fly little planes find ways of dealing with these risks. The most important, which runs through every part of the aviation-oriented press, is the idea that the risks in flying, while greater than those in driving, are also more predictable. By erring on the side of caution in decisions about what weather to fly in, how much gas reserve to allow for, what maneuvers to attempt, pilots tell themselves that they can contain most though not all risks.

This was good enough for the enthusiasts, the Klapmeiers thought, but it would not be enough really to expand the market to people who just wanted to get from here to there in reasonable comfort, safety, and speed.

That was all they had to do: produce a plane that was faster, cheaper, prettier, and dramatically safer than anything the big established companies had come up with. And they convinced themselves that the decade-long collapse of the market gave them just the opportunity they needed. In the business plan they circulated to investors in 1995, they described the difficulties of other companies in the preceding decade as a reason for them to enter the business. "In the past 10 years, the single engine fleet in the U.S. has gone from a total count of 171,900 to 140,000 in 1994. The declining size of the fleet means that demand is outstripping supply.... Cirrus is introducing innovations in safety, performance, comfort, and ease of flying. The attributes will position Cirrus ahead of its competition in general aviation and change the perception of what a new aircraft should be."

Or so they hoped. "The thing about starting a company," Alan Klapmeier said soon after his first SR20 was delivered to his first paying customer (and half a dozen other times too), "is you have to be dumb enough to start, despite all the risks—and then smart enough to keep going." As they did, with help from a surprising quarter.

# The GA Mafia

In 1989, just as the Klapmeiers were discovering how hard it might be to sell their VK-30 kit plane, a career civil servant named Bruce Holmes was trying to decide how he wanted to spend the rest of his working life. Holmes had recently turned forty. He had grown up across the Midwest—early boyhood in South Dakota, adolescence in Illinois, most of high school in Wichita, Kansas, and then on to the University of Kansas. He received his bachelor's, master's, and his doctor of engineering degrees all at Kansas, and all in aeronautical engineering.

Holmes had been interested in planes all his life, taking his first flight in a small plane when he was five years old and soloing when he was in high school. He earned money as a pilot during college in a variety of ways. He towed banners, he flew for commuter airlines, he gave lessons as a flight instructor, he delivered bodies for funeral homes. Holmes began working at NASA in the mid-seventies, while conducting his doctoral research, and became a full-time employee in 1977, when he was twenty-nine. He moved up within the NASA hierarchy, becoming known for his research on "laminar flow," or the way to make the passage of air over an airplane's surface as nonturbulent as possible, for maximum speed, lift, and "slipperiness" in the air.[1] By the time I met him in the late nineties, he was a fit-looking man with a full head of straight, light-brown hair and a genial air. His style of speaking was a combination of an engineer's precision and the sort of "busting paradigms" corporate talk found in *Fast Company* magazine.

Through the late eighties, as the Klapmeiers were discovering that the VK-30 would not sell, Holmes had been meeting with colleagues at NASA headquarters in Langley, Virginia, near Newport News, in weekly gatherings at a neighborhood pizza place. They called themselves the "GA Mafia"—GA as in general aviation—and they discussed the ways that the technical advances so dramatically transforming the worlds of computers and communications might be applied to the relatively stagnant world of air transit. The result of their efforts became widely known and discussed in the aviation community, but they have almost never been discussed in general news outlets. During the very years when news about NASA mainly concerned its struggle to recover from the explosion of the Space Shuttle *Challenger*, in 1986, some of its most creative efforts, and the ones likely to have the greatest impact on the daily lives of the American public, were those undertaken by the GA Mafia.

In the mid-seventies, Jack Olcott, then a senior editor of *Flying* magazine and the chairman of a NASA advisory committee on general aviation, had written a paper recommending development of a "Personal Air Transportation System." By this he meant a new generation of small planes that ordinary travelers could view as a reasonable alternative to the airlines. The planes would have to be safe, comfortable, convenient, and attractive in order to appeal to travelers other than pilots or aviation enthusiasts. But a concerted technological drive should make this possible, he argued. Moreover, economic trends would make it necessary,

since sooner or later the airline-transit system would reach its limits as an efficient, affordable, practical means of getting people
from place to place.

Olcott wrote his paper before the airlines were deregulated and
before the personal-computer age. By the time the members of
the GA Mafia began their speculations, which had been inspired
by Olcott's paper, the deregulated airlines were moving toward a
congested hub-and-spoke pattern, and the computer industry had
shown that it was possible to provide much greater processing
power in much smaller and cheaper packages than had seemed
feasible a decade before.

In the technology industry of the eighties, "Moore's Law" had
become a catchphrase. This was the principle that computing
equipment would roughly double in power, or else drop by half in
price, every eighteen months; it was named after one of the
founders of Intel, Gordon Moore. Moore's law did not apply to the
most costly and complicated single component of an airplane: the
engine. But the process that was bringing ever-cheaper, ever-
smaller, ever more reliable computing equipment to the market
seemed also to have important implications for small airplanes.
Among the many reasons that small-plane flight was more dangerous than travel in big airliners was that small-plane pilots had
less information at their disposal. Their autopilots were more limited. They had a harder time telling where they were and where
they were going. They had less information on the threats they
might run into, from thunderstorms to mountain ridges to other
airplanes nearby. The "flight management" system on a modern
airliner could, with its computers and its backup systems, theoretically control every stage of a flight: takeoff, climb, cruise, descent,
landing dead center on the right runway of the right airport.
Nothing like this was available for small planes.

But sooner or later it would be, the GA Mafia members

thought. Year by year computing power would become cheaper, and so would liquid-crystal display screens like those on laptop computers, and so would the ability to send streams of data to planes in the air. Therefore year by year it should become steadily more feasible for pilots to have a complete, up-to-date, well-displayed rendering of the information that would help them get safely where they wanted to go. In addition, technology originally designed for the military was being turned to civilian use. The first four satellites of what would eventually become a twenty-four-satellite Global Positioning System had gone up in 1978. With signals from the GPS system, pilots—or mariners or soldiers—could navigate by means of "moving map" systems, like those in James Bond movies. When the GA Mafia met in the eighties, the GPS system was still mainly for U.S. military use, and in any case computing power was still too expensive for GPS navigation to be practical for small civilian planes. But Holmes and the others knew that sooner or later the power of GPS would reach the civilian market.

"Looking forward from the eighties you could count on little screens getting cheap, data getting easier to send, digital radios being improved, microprocessors getting faster, satellite navigation getting cheaper, all these other things," Holmes said when I met him at the Newport News airport in southern Virginia. Holmes worked nearby, in NASA's Langley Research Center. I had rented a little Cessna in suburban Washington and made the 140-mile trip in an hour and a half. The trip would have illustrated the practical convenience of small-plane flight—except that the rental plane proved to be a decrepit, thirty-year-old junker whose radios barely worked. This forced me to zigzag around various patches of controlled air space, in which I would have had to make radio contact with an air-traffic controller. Therefore the flight actually illustrated the GA Mafia's original theme: that small planes had to become much better if they were to be of practical use.

Holmes had been sure that they would: "If you projected the technological progress across a twenty-year landscape, from 1990 to 2010, it became obvious that there could be a role for technology in creating a future for GA," he told me that afternoon in Newport News. "And the question was, what was that future and how could NASA help?"

In the late eighties, Holmes began organizing an effort to answer the "future of aviation" question. Apart from his own long-standing personal and professional interest in small airplanes, other forces made this seem a desirable campaign. NASA had suffered serious reverses since the *Challenger* explosion. Congress had reduced its aeronautics budget. Press investigations had revealed obvious management problems. The longstanding culture of the organization was strongly directed toward huge, focused, military-style projects, like the Apollo program and the Shuttle, but few new programs of the sort were in the offing. "Our traditional work has been driven by the sociology and psychology of public projects for mass transport, not personalized travel," Holmes told me. "By what I'll call the Boeing Network culture. In that culture, we talked about the people who operate these vehicles as 'captains' and 'research pilots,' not individuals, and big airports, and ten-to-the-minus-ninth-levels of reliability. [This is how Holmes talks. The term is a "new economy" reference to extremely error-free systems.] They thought the agency's only mission was 'higher, faster, farther,' not lower, slower, and closer to the ground. But within NASA's culture lay the seeds for out-of-the-box thinking about twenty-first century transportation."

Starting shortly after the *Challenger* explosion in 1986, the GA Mafia began its speculative discussions about how great it would be if NASA shifted its attention to small planes. And in 1989, when Holmes had been temporarily transferred from Langley to NASA's headquarters in Washington, he felt he was in a position to act.

That year, Holmes organized a conference of everyone he could think of who might play a role in revitalizing GA. Each of the important groups was known by its acronym. The American Institute of Aeronautics and Astronautics, or AIAA, the leading professional organization. The General Aviation Manufacturers Association, GAMA, the alliance of Cessna, Beech, Piper, and other aircraft companies, plus the supporting members who made engines, instruments, tires, aviation oil. The National Business Aviation Association, NBAA, the corporate-jet people. The Small Aviation Manufacturers Association, SAMA, the low-cost end of the business. The Experimental Aircraft Association, EAA, organizer of each year's Oshkosh convention and leading representative of the kit-plane and experimental movement. The Aircraft Owners and Pilots Association, AOPA, a highly effective lobbying group against efforts to close small airports or impose extra fees on general aviation. NASA itself, plus the Federal Aviation Administration, FAA, which would eventually have to inspect, approve, and certify whatever new planes came onto the market.

Holmes persuaded the varied and often competing groups to join one big conclave, and set its theme: "The role of technology in revitalizing U.S. general aviation." Innocuous as that may sound, it had the potential to be very divisive. Representatives from the pilots' organization, AOPA, and executives from the established small-plane companies, led by Russ Meyer of Cessna, were well into their lobbying campaign to change the tort-liability laws. They feared that attention to any other explanation for the decline in small-plane sales would undercut their case. "I was actually threatened that this would be very risky for my career," Holmes told me. "It was hard to get the key players to participate, because they thought this might threaten their agenda." Holmes managed to assure them that the search for new technologies would complement rather than harm their own efforts to strengthen the industry. The conference concluded with a formal white paper by the American Institute of Aeronautics and Astronautics, in which all affected parties endorsed development of newer, safer, easier-to-fly planes.

After the conference, Holmes received another normal reassignment within NASA, to a job involving space travel rather than airplanes. He "went dormant," as he now puts it, on small-plane questions for several years. But by early 1992, he was back at Langley, as assistant director for aeronautics. His boss in the aeronautics directorate, Roy Harris, was familiar with the discussions of the GA Mafia, and with the increasing potential that computer technology held for small planes. "He told me, 'Bruce, this project is so important, you really should work on it full time,'" Holmes says. Harris told him that he could set up a "skunk works" office within NASA to concentrate on future small-plane development, with a few chosen allies. By all evidence Harris was being sincere in his excitement for the small-plane program, not looking for a subtle way to ease Holmes out of his mainstream-research division.

"It was a difficult decision, to give up an established position, with the largest aeronautics research program in the country, for something that was absolutely unknown," Holmes says. "Most of my peers thought I was nuts to consider it, because of the career risk." But on a springtime evening in 1992, Holmes and his wife were sitting in a hot tub at the home of his friend John Lockhart, a medical doctor and country music player. Holmes had reached his midforties and was wondering if his most interesting days were behind him. "John said, 'This is the future! This is how the future is created!'" Holmes told me. Time was passing—didn't he want to do something while he could?

Yes, he did want to try something new. NASA had just received a new administrator: Daniel Goldin. Goldin had worked at NASA once before, during the glory days of the Apollo program in the early sixties, when he was a young engineer straight out of City College of New York. But after a few years he had joined the defense contractor TRW, and by the early nineties, was in charge of its space technology divisions. At that point he was in his fifties and was a compact man with wavy grey hair.

Goldin came to NASA early in 1992, less than a year before George H. W. Bush had to run for reelection. Appointees who arrive very late in an administration rarely have sweepingly ambitious agendas, since they don't know how long they'll be able to serve. But Goldin had also been thinking about big changes in small-plane travel. By the time of the Oshkosh convention in the late summer of 1992, he was ready to make a speech promising a bright future for general aviation. He told the aviation enthusiasts gathered at Oshkosh that NASA would help make advanced technology practical and affordable for small planes. "I was right there in 1992, as head of an experimental engine company, and I was heartened at the time by what I considered Goldin's pipe dream," a correspondent for Aero-News Network wrote in 2000. "He laid out for us, maybe a hundred industry principals then, what the goal of the agency was: to bring new products to the development stage."[2]

In this supportive environment, Bruce Holmes began organizing what was called the "AGATE project." The acronym stood for Advanced General Aviation Transportation Experiments, and the idea was to stimulate competition among companies to bring new technologies to market. Holmes made a little drawing of the cockpit in an ideal airplane of the future. It would have "highway in the sky" guidance systems, which would give the pilot a graphical path to follow, even if the real view outside were covered by fog. It would have moving maps to let the pilot know exactly where he was—and where the weather, mountains, and other planes might be. It would be comfortable, like a modern car. It would have display panels, rather than old-fashioned "steam gauge" dials, to report the condition of the engine, the electrical system, and anything else the pilot needed to know. "For me that picture became a touchstone," Holmes says. "In a sense the AGATE alliance came out of that sketch—and out of a lot of midnight-oil-burning, weekend-consuming telephone conversations with my fellow thinkers in government, industry, and trade associations."

The organizing idea of the AGATE alliance was like that of the grand conclave Holmes had organized in 1989. He wanted to get every possible participant involved, even those that competed or often disagreed with each other, so that they would all have a stake in the project's success. When the AGATE agreements were signed in 1994, Holmes had brought seventy entities together for the project. These included airplane companies, from the established powers like Cessna to start-ups like Cirrus and Lancair; the engine makers and electronics firms that supplied the industry; university departments of engineering and aeronautics; and the relevant government agencies.

AGATE let out research agreements worth a total of $63 million, authorized by Congress, through the nineties. These went to companies willing to develop demonstration models of the technology that would make small planes better. Visual displays that meant pilots could see and follow a "highway in the sky." New ways to train pilots much more quickly and safely than had seemed possible before. Ways to make planes less likely to crash, and less likely to kill the occupants if they did. Ways to make planes safer in one of the most hazardous flight conditions: an unexpected encounter with ice-filled clouds. New manufacturing techniques, to see if airplane makers could match the revolutionary steps in quality control and lean manufacturing that auto companies had taken in response to the Japanese onslaught. An across-the-board effort to make the costs of flying come down the way the cost of most other high-technology products had since the seventies.

Holmes thought AGATE was making real progress when Dan Goldin, NASA's administrator, began endorsing it in all his speeches, and when congressional committees accepted the argument that better small-plane service could ease impending airline congestion and bring economic opportunity to regions that were hard to reach by highways or railroads. But in a sense the biggest step came in April 1995, when representatives of the companies and agencies in the AGATE consortium met in Lakeland, Florida, to elect a governing committee. "Up until that point, I had been out in front," Holmes says, "but for this to work it had to become an industry-led thing." At the meeting, Stephen Hanvey, an executive from Raytheon, was elected the first chairman of AGATE. "He stepped forward, and I stepped back, and it was quite a moment," Holmes told me. "From playing with the idea, over pizza, we'd come up with a real program, a system of governance, and a plan. And it all went back to Jack Olcott's epiphany in 1974."

While Bruce Holmes was working as Mr. Inside for the small-plane crusade, Dan Goldin served as Mr. Outside. In appearances before Congress and in speeches on the aviation-policy circuit, he placed more and more emphasis on the importance of small-plane programs to NASA—and on the potentially "revolutionary" impact of AGATE and related efforts on the daily lives of the traveling public. His argument had two main themes: that the prevailing airline system was inevitably reaching its limits, and that radically improved small planes could make an important difference to the mass of Americans, not just the existing minority of aviation enthusiasts.

The limits of the existing system were the perverse consequences of success. The historic divide in airline travel occurred in
the late seventies, when Alfred Kahn, an economist from Cornell,
became head of the Civil Aeronautics Board in the Carter administration and undertook a sweeping deregulation.

Before deregulation, airline fares and routes were subject to
extremely detailed government approval and control. If you were
Delta and wanted to offer new service between Atlanta and
Cincinnati, you would have to persuade the Civil Aeronautics
Board to agree. And as part of its approval, the CAB would dictate
how often you could operate the flight, and at what times of day,
and for what fares.

It was an era when commerce in general was far more regulated than it became by the end of the nineties: trucking lines, TV
networks, telephone services were all treated as if they were public utilities at the time. The instinct to regulate was all the stronger
for the airlines, since the CAB's sister bureaucracy, the Federal
Aviation Administration, oversaw the safety and maintenance
standards of the airlines with extremely detailed regulations.
Kahn did not challenge the need for regulation when it came to
safety. But he said that the normal economic aspects of airline
operation—where they flew, how much they charged, how they
competed with each other on price—could be separated from
safety concerns and opened to market forces. He admitted that
there could be a connection between low-budget operations and
decreasing margins of safety. Nonetheless, if the government was
careful to maintain its safety standards, he said, then the rest of
the airlines' operations should be up to them.

The result, as all travelers know, was an air system at the end of
the twentieth century dramatically different from the one at mid-
century. Overall traffic more than doubled, and its rate of increase
was about twice as fast as that of the economy as a whole. The

average fare per mile fell by about one-third.³ But the nature of the market had changed; for efficiency purposes, the airlines had rationalized their routes into a two-tier system: frequent, big-plane connections among the major hubs, and less frequent, more expensive, smaller-plane connections to the surrounding communities. In 1975, Braniff Airlines operated twice-daily nonstops between Austin, Texas, and Washington, D.C., with fancy meal services, Pucci-outfitted flight attendants, but with no frequent-flyer benefits or price competition with other carriers. In 2000, Braniff was out of business, and to get from Washington to Austin passengers took the Reagan National–DFW hub-to-hub flight, followed by a hub-to-spoke trip onward to Austin.

Countless other routes followed the same evolution. Pre-deregulation, there were nonstop flights between New York City and Little Rock. Post-deregulation, Little Rock became a "spoke" and onward travel was inevitably through DFW, the American hub; Cincinnati, the Delta hub; or Memphis, the Northwest hub. In 1978, the major carriers had served a total of 463 cities in the United States. By 1998, they served only 260. The difference was made up by regional and commuter airlines, which of course funneled their passengers into the ever-more crowded hubs.

To the extent that whatever succeeds in the market is the right policy, the shift to hub-and-spoke was the right response to deregulation. Despite initial concerns that cost-cutting would compromise safety, it was hard to find real-world evidence to support that fear. On average, airline flying was far safer twenty years after deregulation than it had been before. And the airlines' essential calculation—that the system that was most efficient for them, in cost per passenger mile, would finally be most attractive to customers, since it would allow the cheapest average fares—turned out to be correct.

What was left out of this equation, of course, was an "unpriced" factor that became all too obvious by the late nineties: the delay and inconvenience the hub-and-spoke system created for the average traveler. The airlines offered huge speed advantages over any other mode of transport—during the minor portion of the overall journey when the passenger was traveling at 400 to 600 miles per hour on the plane. But the speed, convenience, and efficiency of the entire "airline experience" steadily declined. Through the nineties, the range of prices the airlines charged varied more steeply than before. If you could plan two months in advance and buy a nonrefundable ticket, you could go from Dallas to Chicago for one-tenth the cost of a ticket purchased on the day of the flight. The cost of flexible travel therefore rose in the deregulated age.

The external time penalty for getting to and through the hubs rose as well. The NASA researchers had found a distinctive pattern. As the economy developed and per capita income rose, per capita travel rose even faster, and per capita demand for high-speed travel—airlines versus cars or buses—rose faster still.

The point was that air travel was both a cause and a consequence of a more advanced economy. Therefore, if the air system bogged down, at a minimum increasing numbers of people would be annoyed, and it was conceivable that economic productivity would slow as well.

While overall air traffic roughly doubled in the two decades after deregulation, traffic at certain hubs rose far more dramatically. The Cincinnati airport went from 76,000 "operations" (take-offs and landings) in 1978 to 367,000 in 1998. Phoenix went from less than 100,000 to more than 365,000. Charlotte's operations nearly quadrupled. Oakland, Las Vegas, Minneapolis–St. Paul, Salt Lake City, and others increased substantially.[4] For the airlines, this was like any other scaling-up of an industrial process. But for travelers it had the obvious consequences:

- a longer and less predictable route to the airport, because of chronically jammed traffic and the need to allow for occasional severe slowdowns;
- slower and less predictable progress through the airport— check-in, security, baggage handling;
- more crowded conditions for the airplanes themselves at the airports and on the hub-to-hub airways, leading to slower effective travel times even as the airplanes have theoretically become faster. Between 1980 and 2000 the *scheduled* air-travel time between LaGuardia and DFW increased by thirty minutes, or 20 percent, as the airlines allowed for all the time penalties of congestion: waiting to push back from the gate, waiting to get on the runway, waiting for clearances to land;
- a far greater probability of flights not meeting even these slower scheduled times. Past-schedule arrivals set a record in 1999, which was broken in 2000. In August 2000, an exasperated airport official was quoted in the *New York Times* about the essence of the situation: "'As long as a passenger is willing to get on an airplane, airlines tend not to think of how long it takes you to get there, the parking, the hassles, getting through the terminal,' said Todd Hauptli, senior vice president for policy and government affairs of the American Association of Airport Executives. 'All they care about is that you get in one of their seats.'"[5]

"Since October 10, 1998, I've been keeping a detailed log of all my travel, with a stopwatch and everything," Bruce Holmes told me, about two years after starting this project. When he left his home or office, he would enter the exact time in his Palm Pilot. When he got to the airport, he'd make another entry. When the plane departed, another entry. Another for any stop the plane made along the way; another when the plane reached his destination airport; and a final entry when Holmes reached the destination he really had in mind—a hotel, a meeting site, his home if he was returning from the road. And at each step of the journey, Holmes calculated and entered the distance he was actually traveling—for example, from his home airport in Hampton Roads, Virginia, to the US Airways hub in Charlotte, and then from Charlotte to wherever the next flight went. "You know the productivity expert, W. Edwards Deming?" Deming was an American consultant whose program for increasing productivity began with minute measurements of each stage of a factory's production process. "My friends used to say, 'Deming would be proud.'"

"When the trip is over, I calculate it against the great circle distance [direct route] and work out the effective speed, from doorstep to destination," he told me. Using flight-planning software, he then calculates how long the flight would have taken if he had been able to use a small plane and travel direct from the airport closest to his home to the one closest to his destination. (Because the airplane world runs on knots rather than miles-per-hour, he works out all these figures in knots, which again are about 15 percent higher than miles per hour.)

What Holmes found, after tabulating results from 76 airline trips, was just how slow hub-and-spoke airline travel had become. For trips of 500 miles or less, what Holmes called his "doorstep to destination" speed averaged 75 knots, or somewhat faster than he could have gone by car. The car, of course, would have been less expensive, and allowed him more flexibility in when to travel and return. His worst short trip was one from Boston to Newport News, Virginia, when a string of thunderstorms caused delays throughout the hub-and-spoke system. That took 27 hours, for an average speed of 15 knots. For trips of 1,000 miles, he averaged 125 knots. For trips of 2,000 miles, he averaged 200 knots. These longer trips were obviously faster than driving, but not faster than they would have been in improved small planes. "The ugly truth," as he put it, was that "we are a nation that is slowing down, not speeding up, during an age when time is the scarce commodity for all of us."[6]

NASA's way of depicting the same trend was to calculate average travel times, based on the airlines' own schedules, assuming no unusual slowdowns. This was the basis of Daniel Goldin's claim that for distances less than 400 miles the effective speed of airlines was no better than that in a car.

If you were traveling from one big city to another, you had to cope with congestion at the major airports; and if you were traveling between smaller cities, you endured the penalties of indirect routing. Based on these trends, Goldin concluded that for a growing category of travelers and routes, some alternative to airlines could be faster door to door. No other mode of travel would be faster than a modern jetliner from takeoff to touchdown, but the speed advantages of direct routing, and the reduced congestion at either end, might amount to a more convenient, less harassing, less wasteful overall system of transportation.[7]

The pressure for a better alternative to the airlines was likely to increase, Goldin contended, as part of his argument that NASA should play an active role in improving the air-transport system. Population was growing. Wealth was growing. Therefore the likely demand for transportation would steadily grow. Although the Internet might in theory eliminate the need for face-to-face meeting, at least initially it coincided with a continued surge in travel. And what Bruce Holmes called a "third wave" in migration—of people to attractive remote areas, wanting to commute at least occasionally to cities for work—would increase travel pressure, and in a way the hub airlines were particularly ill-equipped to serve. The first wave, in the nineteenth century, was farm to city; then city to suburbs through most of the twentieth century; then for significant numbers of people suburbs to rural areas.

Highways had revolutionized travel when they essentially tripled the door-to-door speed of the previous transportation standard, horses; commercial airliners had revolutionized travel by tripling the effective door-to-door speed of trains. But because of congestion airlines were now losing their time advantage over cars.

"The automobile increased the speed of doorstep to destination travel to over fifty to sixty miles per hour," Goldin said in his stump speech about the need for small airplanes. "Unfortunately, that's where we've been stuck for the past three decades. In fact, the average speed of interstate highway travel has been slowly decreasing during the past decade. Now, airlines are slowing down, too." Moreover, "we envision advances in speed for personal transportation so an individual's average daily radius of action will increase by a factor of ten—from 30 to 50 miles in the age of the interstate highway and hub-spoke system ... to 300 to 500 miles in the age of the Small Aircraft Transportation System."[8]

Bruce Holmes had a complementary stump speech, which said:

*Personal speed* (or speed at your personal command) is the most important factor in transportation advancement, because *personal transportation* is the most *democratizing* form of transportation. The *automobile* produced the most revolutionary advancements in civilization for these very reasons. *Somehow,* we have forgotten the important lessons of the automobile as we have begun teaching our children that public transportation is the "only or best" kind of green transportation choice....

Unfortunately, *advancements in personal transportation stopped* in about 1950 at an average speed of about 60 miles per hour with the completion of the InterState Highway System.... *No public transportation mode in history* has ever dominated in mode share following the introduction of practical personal transportation alternatives. The prime example is the demise of the rails as a dominant mode share following the introduction of the automobile.[9]

In attempting to determine whether a new generation of small airplanes, serving an improved and expanded network of small airports, could realistically play a part in future mass transportation, the NASA team tried to assess, first, the needs that the established airlines were likely to leave unfilled.[10] The airline trend had been toward ever more intense concentration on hub-spoke routings. The economic incentives of the deregulated age had driven them in that direction, and NASA believed there was little reason to expect the incentives or trend to change.

The next step was determining how much of the frustrated desire for mobility new and improved small planes might satisfy— and whether it was even worth considering that any substantial number of Americans could be expected to fly planes themselves. As a long-time pilot, Bruce Holmes had a bias toward thinking that lots of people would enjoy flying if they had the right introduction to it. But NASA based its plans on the level-headed assumption that even if the population of pilots grew, as airplanes became safer, simpler, and more affordable, people willing and able to fly their own planes would still be the distinct minority.[11] A new small-plane transportation system would have to offer advantages to the vast nonpilot civilian majority if it were to make any broad public sense. In practice this would mean the creation of what was still the missing type of airplane: small planes that had the speed, safety, comfort, and comparatively low price to serve as a national air-taxi fleet.

More specifically, NASA's goals, similar to those of the Klapmeiers, were: Small airplanes should be *safer*, so that normal, non-risk-taking people could reasonably imagine trusting their lives to them. They should be *faster*, so they could in effect offer another tripling of speed relative to the highway. In practice this meant a target of 200 miles per hour cruising speed. They should be *more efficient* and *less environmentally harmful*, using less fuel, creating less pollution, and generating less noise. They should be far *simpler* to fly and more consistent in their operations, much like cars that vary little from one rental site to another. And they should be *radically cheaper and more reliable*, following the examples of the high-tech industry and even auto manufacturers, with their quality revolution of the eighties and nineties.

By the late nineties, Daniel Goldin was ready to propose specific performance benchmarks for the new generation of planes. The goals had different details at different times, but this is the way Goldin put them in a speech in 1998:

*Goal One*: We want to reduce the aircraft accident rate by a factor of five within ten years, and by a factor of ten within twenty years.

*Goal Two*: We want to reduce emissions of future aircraft by a factor of three within ten years, and by a factor of five within twenty years.

*Goal Three*: We want to reduce the perceived noise levels of future aircraft by a factor of two from today's subsonic aircraft within ten years, and by a factor of four within twenty years.

*Goal Four*: While maintaining safety and reliability, we want to triple the aviation system throughput, in all weather conditions, within ten years.

*Goal Five*: Reduce the cost of air travel by 25 percent within ten years, and by 50 percent within twenty years.

*Goal Six*: Reduce the travel time to the Far East and Europe by 50 percent within twenty years and do so at today's subsonic ticket prices.

*Goal Seven*: Invigorate the general aviation industry, delivering 10,000 aircraft annually within ten years, and 20,000 within twenty years, back to a level we have not seen since the seventies!

*Goal Eight*: Provide next-generation design tools and experimental aircraft to increase design confidence, and cut the development cycle time for aircraft by a minimum of 50 percent.[12]

Achieving these goals would in turn require a host of intermediate accomplishments—in new safety equipment, new production techniques, new ways of cutting costs. These, too, Goldin, Holmes, and others elaborated in their talks.[13] NASA also set targets for the coverage and convenience a small-plane network should achieve. To make a difference, a new system should serve every part of the United States that was more than fifty miles, or an hour's drive, whichever was less, from a major hub airport. "The NASA Aerospace Technology Enterprise Goal is to reduce travel times by half in ten years and more in twenty-five years," Holmes says. "Fortunately, more than 98 percent of the U.S. population lives within a thirty-minute drive of over 5,000 public-use landing facilities. This infrastructure is an untapped national resource for mobility."

Although these small airports are far more evenly and conveniently spaced across the country than the large hubs, not enough of them are equipped for all-weather operation. The most important all-weather component is a "precision landing system," which lets pilots safely descend for a landing even if clouds are within a few hundred feet of the ground. (Large airliners are equipped with "Category III" precision landing systems, which let the planes land safely even if clouds or fog reach all the way to ground level.)

Some 1,200 of the nation's public airports already have precision landing systems; of them, about 400 have control towers and full air-traffic control services. In his speeches, Holmes argued that if landing systems and air-traffic control services were installed at many more airports, the result would be a dramatic increase in the practicality of small-plane travel:

> According to these figures, in the late nineties general aviation conducted a total of 37 million "operations" (takeoffs and landings) per year. If landing systems and control services were improved at the 5,400 largest public airports, operations could go to more than 500 million a year, without a single new runway being built except at the currently most-crowded hubs.

So the NASA of the late nineties had its plans laid. Different airplanes. Better engines. A bigger network of improved airports. Connected to these major goals were a variety of subsidiary ones. Faster, surer, more natural ways of training pilots. Radically simpler navigation systems, to avoid the disorientation and inadvertent flight into bad weather that are the main sources of small-plane crashes. Improvements in manufacturing, so that aircraft companies could learn from car makers, much as they had during World War II.

But there remained a problem. What, exactly, could NASA do about any of this? The organization had no direct operating responsibility for certifying airplanes, training pilots, or equipping airports. Was this all just a way of building a new bureaucratic empire: of finding extra jobs for NASA when space exploration seemed to have lost its public allure?

Some of NASA's critics inside and outside the government said that this was exactly the motive. At aviation shows through the late nineties, Bruce Holmes put on *Crossfire*-style debates with the renowned airplane designer Burt Rutan. Most of these sessions consisted of Rutan denouncing the idea that the government could subsidize innovation.

But through the history of aviation, governments had frequently played a role in shaping the industry's evolution—specifically including sponsoring innovators through competitions and initial contracts. Government contracts to deliver air mail kept small aircraft companies alive at the dawn of the industry; the Wright brothers' first big sale was to the military. And Holmes and Goldin both argued that if any government agency were to address the logjam in air travel, NASA was the right one. The analogy would be to the government's role in medical research and health. The National Institutes of Health sponsor basic research on a wide variety of biological and medical problems. Most of the experiments have no immediate practical payoff; a few lead to breakthroughs in diagnosis, prevention, or cure. When these innovations enter normal medical application, Medicare and other federal agencies help pay for them, and the Food and Drug Administration supervises the new drugs involved.

So with air transportation, officials at NASA reasoned. The Federal Aviation Administration and the National Transportation Safety Board had their hands more than full trying to ensure that the system operated day by day and year by year. That left it to NASA, which after all was the National *Aeronautics* and Space

Administration, to look beyond the immediate operating challenges toward future possibilities. Bruce Holmes likes to say NASA
should be in the business of "disruptive change," taking risks and
being willing to make mistakes. The FAA and NTSB, by contrast,
are supposed to err constantly on the side of caution, established
procedures, and a belt-plus-suspenders bias in favor of extra
safety.

"The FAA's 'mainstream line of business' is to continuously
improve the safety and services in the hub-and-spoke system for
the airlines and their customers," Holmes puts it. "That's what
they're chartered to do by the Congress and the public. NASA has
and should have the ability to explore outside of the bounds that
are constrained by regulation, certification, existing airspace
architectures and procedures. Once the technology starts to
become proven, the FAA picks up the heavy lifting."

Goldin was frequently quoted on this theme as well. "The FAA
doesn't have the capacity to invent," he said in the fall of 2000
(after Congress had briefly "zeroed out" NASA funds for small-air-
plane research, which were then restored).[14] By contrast, at NASA
"we don't want to fund anything that's not revolutionary."[15] In his
debates with Holmes at aviation conventions, Burt Rutan would
razz NASA by saying that the Goldin administration had been in
office longer than it took the original space program to go from the
launch of *Sputnik* (in 1957) to John Glenn's ride as the first American to circle the earth (1962). Holmes would reply that during
those apparently idle "Goldin years" of the nineties, NASA had in
fact carefully laid the foundation for dramatic progress in flight,
even though the press and public paid practically no attention.

# The Teardrop and the Cigar Tube

By the early nineties, the Klapmeier brothers thought they were making progress. The kit-plane business had proved to be harder than they expected. But it had given them operating experience, and the contract with Israviation helped cover their payroll as they planned their next step. They believed they were ready for a direct move toward what they'd always thought of as the real goal: designing, certifying, and selling the first genuinely new airplane the business had seen in a generation.

"When we introduced our first kit plane 1987, it got us magazine covers, and people did recognize that there was something interesting happening here," Alan Klapmeier told me during one meeting. It was an unusually warm fall day in Duluth—so warm that swarms of bees had surrounded all the downtown restaurants, and after trying to sit on the deck and look at sailboats on the lake we were driven indoors.

"At that point we still didn't think we had to look for outside money. We believed that the development time [for a certified plane] would be short enough that we could just wrap up the kit company in a profitable way, and develop our new airplanes. We weren't sure exactly what our company would look like. But we always believed that we were going to build certified production airplanes. We thought it was a good market, and we felt that the rest of the industry was ignoring it. Not to the benefit of the industry, but certainly to our benefit, they continued to do that for the next ten or fifteen years.

"So the attention we got after we introduced the kit convinced us that we should continue to put our own time and our own family money into it. We were theoretically paying ourselves $36,000 a year, but most of that was deferred. We were actually taking home $12,000. We were eating macaroni and cheese and living at the farm. All that early 'deferred income,' by the way, disappeared the first time we went to a bank and looked for a line of credit. They said, 'Aha! You've got to make the balance sheet look better. If this money is owed to you, it's gone.' Obviously we now wish that we'd worked it out so that someday we'd get paid."

The Klapmeiers' decision to try the certified market constituted an enormous commitment. Preparing a plane that would pass the FAA's standards would mean years of building, testing, and refining prototypes, and an investment of many millions of dollars. But exactly what sort of plane should they build?

If working capital had been no object, they could simply have done by themselves what Israviation had contracted to do. That is, they could have built a turbine-powered plane, priced at a million dollars or more, and positioned it as a faster, cheaper, more elegant alternative to the prevailing generation of business planes.

But working capital was an obstacle, then and at every subsequent moment of Cirrus's corporate existence. So the brothers thought instead that they would start with a challenge to the other end of the existing aircraft product line. Their plane would have a piston engine, rather than turbine power; it would be driven by a plain old propeller; and it would hold four people rather than six or eight. But it would, as they imagined it, be so different from anything then on the market that it would signal a new age for small planes.

This strategy, in turn, involved a variety of subsequent decisions. The Klapmeiers decided early that theirs would be a "plastic plane"—one whose body and wings were made of composite materials, mainly fiberglass, rather than of aluminum. This was the same decision they had made for their first, experimental plane, the VK-30, in the eighties, and it had obvious advantages for a small firm like theirs.

Through the twentieth century, the dominant materials for airplane construction had evolved in clear phases. First there were cloth-covered wood frames; then lightweight wood construction; then, in time for World War II, mass production of aluminum airplanes. By the end of the twentieth century, aluminum was still the dominant material for all flying craft except the most exotic, highest-performance military airplanes. Those planes used titanium and other metals with very high strength-to-weight ratios, plus strong, light, and expensive composite materials like carbon or graphite fiber.

For most civilian and military airplanes, aluminum was attractive principally because it was light. Compared with other reasonably priced materials, aluminum was stronger than anything else that weighed as much, and lighter than anything else that was as strong. Therefore most planes in the GA fleet had aluminum in all the places where the strength-to-weight ratio was particularly important: for the structural components of an airplane's wing and fuselage, for the airplane's skin, or for "control surfaces" like ailerons and elevators.

But for the kind of plane the Klapmeiers had in mind, and for the kind of small, capital-poor company Cirrus still was, aluminum had disadvantages too. The central problem was that if you could not afford to invest in very expensive machine tools, like those that Boeing might use, it was hard to form the aluminum into any kind of interesting or sophisticated shape.

"Most small metal airplanes are built essentially like mailboxes," says Mike Van Staagen, a refugee from architecture school who played a major part in designing the Cirrus's interior "They are two-dimensional curves. And then they're kind of hammered together and have harsh angles to them." Even the fuselages of modern airliners are shaped like enormous cigar tubes, but their dimensions are so large that they can be (comparatively) roomy inside. Small airplanes are shaped like small cigar tubes, and their dimensions make their interiors surprisingly cramped.

A nicer shape for moving through the air, while also maximizing interior space, would be more like a teardrop than a cigar tube. This combines the smallest possible external drag with the largest possible internal dimensions. But it requires forming the airplane's structure into "complex curves" rather than simple tubes. "That's where composite technology comes in," Van Staagen says. "It lets you build wide cabins that are more slippery through the air. It also gives you a nice material to work with from a designer's point of view. You can have a lot of sex appeal, you have nice pleasing lines. Just like with modern cars, you can have a flowing design, and the air *loves* to be parted and put back together very nicely. That is simply why you get the faster speeds with composite design."

Aluminum had other problems, too, from the Klapmeiers' perspective. Again because of the difficulties of molding large pieces of metal into complicated shapes, aluminum airplanes are usually assembled from a variety of small pieces, which in turn are fastened together with rivets. This means that the plane's surface inevitably is marked with seams and with rivet heads—that is, with countless small irregularities that create drag in the air.

All these forces pushed the Klapmeiers to accept the weight penalty and use composites for their airplane.[1] They knew, too, that for a small company trying to sneak its way into the airplane business, composites were a cheaper way to begin than metal would be. And they paid particular attention to the design advantages of composite construction. If this was supposed to be an "exciting," "different" plane, it would need the advantages composites brought. The ease of shaping composite materials could make the plane seem larger inside, while its aerodynamic exterior could make it "slipperier" in the air so it could move faster than existing models with a comparable engine.

Viewed from above, the cabin of the plane they had in mind would essentially have a teardrop shape. At the widest point of the cabin, it would measure forty-nine inches from one interior wall to the other. This would be five to ten inches wider than existing four-place planes, and it would give the Cirrus the feeling of a comfortable sports car. Each person in the front seat would have room to sit and shift around without bumping his neighbor. The interior would also be taller than normal, fifty inches from floor to ceiling, so that even tall people would not hit their heads. The guiding idea through the design process was to make the plane as plush-seeming, comfortable, and well appointed as the Lexus and Infiniti cars that had appeared on the market in the late eighties. "One of the things I like is that when this plane comes out, there will be thousands of people going to the psychiatrist," Alan Klapmeier told me. "'Doctor, I can't understand it—my [existing] plane just got ugly!'"

"We knew we could get the performance we wanted out of the plane by using composites," said Paul Johnston, the free spirit who was Cirrus's chief engineer when I first met him. "We spent a lot of time over in Germany, because at that time they were the only ones who seriously had done the job of producing composite airplanes in quantity. They'd been producing gliders at a rate of an airplane a day. That was what we wanted to learn."

One challenge Cirrus faced in learning from past practice in composites was that the composite business is split into two very different parts. Most of the high-volume output is in the boat-building industry, with some allies among companies that make RVs or modifications for cars and trucks. The other is the defense industry, where exotic planes are built for tens of millions of dollars apiece.

"These two ends of the spectrum in the composite industry are each very interesting," Mike Van Staagen, who designed much of the plane's interior, told me. "One end is the cheaper fiberglass boats. They are thrown together very inexpensively, quickly. People have built many, many, many in this process, so that now you can have a ten-thousand-dollar boat. And that is an incredible accomplishment. They're built just about like hot tubs. There is a fiberglass technology out there that is rapid, fast, and loose.

"On the other end, you have your Department of Defense contractors. You've got missiles and billion-dollar airplanes being fabricated out of composites. That's the technology we're after! But we had to build it with a boat-type mentality—high volume, low cost. We had to end up in the middle somewhere. When you're building boats and fiberglass bathtubs you're not worried that much about strength, longevity, and weight. In the Department of Defense side, you're interested in very high performance, doing things that have never been done before. We want 'em both. We want to have the lightweight, incredibly efficient composite structure, but we want to be able to build it very inexpensively."

Cirrus knew what the plane would be made of. Next, what should it look like? "Unlike with metal, composites didn't limit the shapes you could consider," Paul Johnston says. "So we knew you had a fairly free-form shape. So the next step was to look at those inside-the-cockpit issues." That is, the company would plan the outside of the plane by starting with the inside.

This was not exactly the approach the GA industry had taken before. The interiors, seats, and cabin finishings of the typical small plane had obviously been the last items on the designers' priority lists. The idea at Cirrus was to start with an interior that would be spacious and luxurious, and then build a fuselage around that.

"We spent a lot of time, early, thinking about the inside," Paul Johnston says. "For example, everyone will tell you that a Mooney 201 is a small, cramped airplane." The Mooney is the Corvette of small planes—always faster than competitive models, but also smaller-feeling inside, as if you were getting into a racing car. Johnston continues: "But if you measure a Mooney's internal dimensions, it's not that small. So why does it feel that way? Well, the instrument panel is very close to you. And the panel is very high, so you feel like you're sitting down in a bucket. And the sills of the side windows are high, so you're sitting down in this hole and you feel claustrophobic. The plane *feels* smaller than it is.

"So we would go from plane to plane asking ourselves what felt good about this plane, what felt bad about this plane, then actually measuring and seeing what things were making us feel good or bad about this airplane. The Bonanza is considered a 'big' airplane. It's not dimensionally that big, but the windows are lower, which gives you that open feeling. And your head is not too close to the wall. So we took the idea of a big cockpit and built full-scale mockups out of foam and plywood. One of the engineers was very tall, maybe six-seven, with a long torso, so we put headsets on him and used him as a guide."

Mike Van Staagen, himself just over 6'4'', says, "The cockpit is everything. One like this had never been done before. That is the easiest and biggest target to hit."

"The first step was to get the interior volume the way we wanted, and the windows the way we wanted, with lots of visibility," says Paul Johnston. Visibility became one of the guiding principles of the designers. "Visibility plays a huge part in comfort," Dale Klapmeier says. "It's far more 'comfortable' to fly in an airplane you can see out of than one you're trying to get your head up over the panel."

Paul Johnston says that, in the interests of creating a spacious plane, the normal instincts of the airplane designer had to be resisted at certain points. "Usually there's a step where you rake everything back, make it very streamlined, make it look like it's going a hundred miles an hour on the ground," he says. "But soon you realize that you're giving up everything you fought for in the

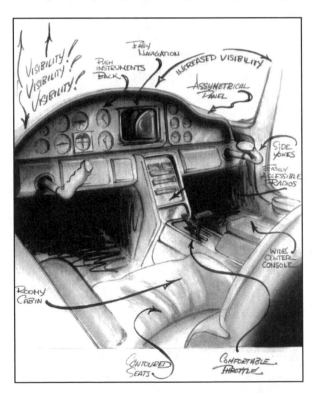

"Visibility!" The concept drawing for the SR20's interior.

cabin. Initially people had thought that the cabin was a little bulbous, protruding, not as sleek as everyone wanted it. But when you got in the airplane you realized what you were getting for that. Aerodynamically it was not costing us anything, and then it became a good-looking thing."

After hearing "Visibility, Visibility" as the slogan for the airplane's design, Mike Van Staagen produced a concept drawing of how the cockpit should look and feel.

Once the plane was finished, everyone at Cirrus claimed to be happy with the open, airy look of the SR20's cockpit, but many of those involved in the design process remember it as a continual series of arguments, reconsiderations, and compromises. The major combatants were often the two Klapmeier brothers themselves. Alan was increasingly involved in his Mr. Outside duties of raising money and generating publicity, and Dale remained Mr. Inside, concerned with engineering and operations. But each had strong views about how the plane should look. As a rule Dale was skeptical of features that would make the plane seem *too* unconventional, or any slower than it could potentially be. Alan, meanwhile, was most likely to challenge any designer's or engineer's assertion that a certain feature was impractical or too hard to work out. "To get Alan in a tizzy, all one has to say is that 'it can't be done,'" one veteran of the discussions told me. "You'd have a full-fledged debate and raised voices in a matter of seconds if he thought otherwise. And you would not win. That was uncomfortable at times. But in the end, Alan's 'I can do anything' demeanor prevailed most of the time, making engineering go back to sharpen the pencils or pickax."

Through this process Dale Klapmeier became known for a refrain of "over my dead body." This was his initial response to most suggestions that the plane depart from the design norms for small airplanes—by replacing the conventional "yoke," a device like a steering wheel, with a small side-stick with which the pilot would steer the plane, or by arranging the cockpit so that it resembled an automobile, with distinct "driver" and "passenger" layouts of the front seat. (Normal airplanes are laid out so that the left and right seats in the front are as similar as possible, so that two pilots can sit together for training or to share the workload.)

Mike Van Staagen was frequently on the other side of these arguments. Over the months it took to work out the design, nearly a dozen other engineers, designers, and stress analysts weighed in with the view that the SR20 should look as *un*like existing planes as possible.[2] Sometimes the designers would pretend not to hear instructions from their nominal superiors and would proceed on their own course. For instance, Van Staagen deliberately laid out the fuselage so that the backseat passengers had four or five inches more leg room than Dale had thought necessary. This way very tall people, like Van Staagen, could sit in the backseat and not bump their knees. One evening Dale walked by Van Staagen's computer station and said, "I understand that you want to make this bigger," pointing at the seat layouts Van Staagen was working on.

"Yeah, that's what I'm doing," Van Staagen replied.

"No, you're not."

"Why?"

"Because there's no need to make it any bigger." With that Dale Klapmeier walked Van Staagen out to his Chevy Blazer in the parking lot and measured the distance between front and rear seats. It was five inches shorter than what Van Staagen had in mind.

"I got in the back of the Blazer, and I couldn't fit with my legs facing forward," Van Staagen said afterwards. He went back to his computer, figured out just how much room it would take for someone like him to sit comfortably in the back of the airplane, and designed that much space in. By the time anyone noticed his insubordination, prototypes were flying, and it was too late to do anything about it. When the plane eventually hit the market, reviews noted that it was about the first four-place plane to be comfortable for backseat passengers. "And I am convinced," Van Staagen says, "that we won many more customers with that sense of internal comfort than we drove away by the two knots of speed we may have lost." He added, "What I like most about Dale is that if you can convince him that there is a better choice, he'll be behind you 100 percent and he'll forget that he was once opposed to it." Dale now says that he is delighted with the comfort of the plane.

And so the arguments went on, leading to an accumulation of small decisions for an unconventional, comfort-oriented approach. The plane did end up with a side-stick rather than a yoke. The main result of this is to clear a broad, open area in front of "driver" and "passenger" alike in the front seat.[3] The cabin ended up being several inches wider than would have been sensi-

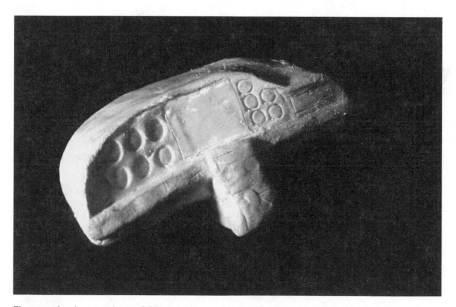

First crude clay mockup of SR20 instrument panel.

ble if maximum speed were the main criterion. "Because of the composites, we could push the cabin out a few more inches," Mike Van Staagen says. That is, a composite plane could have a teardrop shape, with a wide cabin area and narrow nose and tail. "That meant you could have the center console for each person, not like a movie theater where you're fighting for control of it." The part of the fuselage containing the back seats became several inches wider than originally planned, after aerodynamic studies showed that this widening wouldn't really add air resistance or slow the plane down. "My belief is that people don't want to *touch* each other when they're sitting," Van Staagen says; the extra width created a no-touch zone between the two rear passengers. The instrument panel ended up being three or four inches farther away from the pilot than normal, increasing the sense of space— and the side of it facing the "passenger" ended up with very few controls.

"We had a fight over the temptation to just make the instrument panel as big as possible, all the way across, so you could cram all sorts of dials and gauges in there," Alan Klapmeier says. "The pilots think they want all that extra stuff. But if you put too much stuff in there it just makes the passenger feel bad. They feel they should be doing something. So we deliberately made a panel that is angled toward the driver, just like in every car you'll see. The only reason this seemed unusual is that so many aircraft designers refuse to look at things from the nonpilot's point of view."

After the clay mockup, the next version of the interior showed a further step toward an automotive "driver/passenger" look. And then, in the production model, all the features Van Staagen and Johnston were pushing for were even further emphasized—visibility, recessed features, asymmetrical panel.

Working model of SR20 cockpit.

At the end of this process, the Cirrus team thought it had a plane that would be modern and comfortable, so it could appeal to people who'd grown used to the improved cars of the nineties. It would use advanced materials that would help it attain speeds high enough to be an attractive alternative to airlines and interstate highways. It would be priced so as to compete not with exist-

Interior of production–model SR20.

ing Bonanzas and Mooneys, at $300,000 and sharply up, but at roughly half that much, to compete with expensive RVs and vacation cottages, as a way to bring more buyers into the market.

But there was one other factor without which all the rest would be meaningless. The plane had to be safer, and to seem much safer, than those currently available. Otherwise, most members of the public would not even consider buying or riding in it.

To the public that is generally terrified of small airplanes, "safety" boils down to "staying out of those death traps." But to understand how people now involved in flying make their peace with the current levels of risks, and why they think the public might ever accept travel in small planes, let's return to the fundamental issues of what makes flight safe or dangerous.

# The Plane with the Parachute

Stepping onto a modern commercial airliner is, statistically, an almost risk-free action. In many recent years, the chance of dying from anything other than natural medical causes while aboard an airliner has been zero or close to it, since those years passed with few or no airline fatalities. The modern crashes that do occur are, in a sense, terrifying precisely because of their rarity. As the predictable causes of large-airplane failure have been identified and reduced or eliminated, what remains are: crashes no one can yet explain, like the explosion of TWA Flight 800 off Long Island in 1996; crashes apparently arising from deliberate suicidal actions by the pilots, like the SilkAir crash in Indonesia in 1997 and perhaps the EgyptAir crash of 1999; and crashes that come at the end of a long chain of low-probability events. The crash of ValuJet flight 592 in the Florida Everglades, in 1996, apparently involved just such a sequence of misfortunes, each of which was individually so unlikely that no one had foreseen them happening in this combined form.[1] The seeming randomness of modern airline disaster is both alarming and, in an odd way, reassuring. It is alarming as a reminder of the role of pure chance in determining life and death. It is reassuring in an icy, logical sense: the events have become so rare that there is no clear pattern to connect them.

The situation with small planes is the reverse. Accidents are much more common among general aviation planes than for airliners. But because their causes are so much more obvious than those of recent airline disasters, and because those causes, once known, are in theory largely preventable, pilots consider this objectively more dangerous activity less terrifying than one in which the risks are entirely out of one's control.

This attitude has its elements of simple denial, but it also is based on the well-understood patterns of small-plane accidents. Each year the Air Safety Foundation publishes its "Nall Report," analyzing the GA crashes of the preceding year. (The report is named for Joe Nall, a member of the National Transportation Safety Board, who died in an airplane crash in Venezuela in 1989.) The reports have shown the number of crashes, of deaths, and of crashes per flying hour declining steadily through the nineties and into the new century. But the causes of the crashes have been consistent.

Year in and year out, two conditions have led all other causes of GA crashes. One is weather problems, especially "visual flight into instrument conditions." This is what has become known as the "John Kennedy scenario," in which pilots not fully trained to fly in the clouds inadvertently find themselves there and are unable to avoid a spiraling dive and crash.[2] In 1998, there were 341 fatal GA accidents. Of these, 54 were attributed to weather problems, including 39 with the "Kennedy scenario." (The remaining weather-related accidents were caused by "severe weather," mainly thunderstorms or freezing clouds that covered a plane with ice, and instrument-rated pilots who lost control of their planes while in the clouds.)

The other main type of danger for small planes is "low-level maneuvering flight." A plane is maneuvering when it is doing something other than normal point-to-point cruising. "Low level" flight is generally considered to be anything less than 1,000 feet above the ground. The closer a plane is to the ground, the smaller the margin of error for its pilot. What goes wrong when a pilot loses control and a plane enters a stall or spin is that the plane suddenly descends. During primary training, pilots are taught to recover from a stall with a loss of only a few hundred feet of altitude. Those who take spin training learn to recover from a spin by the time the plane has lost roughly 1,000 feet of altitude. All of this is fine if a plane starts the spin at 5,000 feet above ground level, but not if it is, say, 800 feet above the airport making its final turn before landing.

In 1998, maneuvering incidents, mainly at low level, accounted for 63 of the 341 fatal crashes. "Some of these accidents occurred during legitimate activities such as aerial applications, banner towing, and law enforcement," the Nall Report for that year observes. "These operations require low, slow flight and considerable mission-related division of attention .... These operations carry some inherent risk and demand skill and vigilance from the pilot." But other accidents, it said:

> occurred during buzzing or low-level aerobatics. Many involved a degree of recklessness that makes it difficult to term them 'accidents' in a true sense. No increase in proficiency can prevent such accidents. Only a change in attitude on the part of the pilots involved can reduce the problem. Such antics are not the mark of a skilled pilot—only a potentially dead one.[3]

Together weather problems and maneuvering flight accounted for 117 of the 341 fatal crashes in 1998, just over one-third. The other significant causes were: mechanical failures, mainly of the engine or propeller, nineteen fatal crashes; midair collisions, nearly all within a few miles of an airport or during formation-flight, eleven; "fuel mismanagement," that is, running out of gas, nine; and problems during the approach for a landing, about twenty (excluding those that occurred during the approach but were mainly attributed to bad weather). In 1998, two fatal crashes were blamed on "pilot incapacitation," one from a heart attack and another when a pilot blacked out after doing high-G aerobatic maneuvers. Four people were killed when they walked into spinning propellers. Only one fatal crash in the entire year was traced to a pilot's use of alcohol or drugs. In a typical year, fewer than 1 percent of all GA crashes are thought to be due to alcohol. And of the 341 GA crashes that led to fatalities in 1998, fifty-four of them were in homebuilt airplanes. This is a somewhat confusing statistic, since home-built crashes that involved low-level maneuvering or fuel exhaustion are also tabulated in those categories. Still, the disproportionate risk associated with home-built (and much less carefully regulated) aircraft emphasizes the larger point: that small-plane risk factors follow more predictable patterns than those for the airlines.

These general patterns of risk in flying are familiar to anyone who has finished pilot training. And as they survey this list of hazards, most pilots reach two contradictory-sounding conclusions. On the one hand, they know that small planes can be very dangerous, and that by flying they inevitably expose themselves to risk. Long months can pass between fatal airline crashes, while on average there is one fatal small-plane accident in the United States every day.

But on the other hand, pilots who study safety records also observe that the most important risk factors are, at least in theory, subject to mitigation if not complete control. Flying when the weather looks dangerous, performing needless low-level maneuvers, trying to go too far on a tank of gas, taking off without a careful preflight check—accidents originating from these sources are different from, say, being struck on the road by a drunk driver who careens across the median. The difference is that a driver is always vulnerable to the recklessness of others, whereas a careful pilot could in principle avoid the major flying hazards.

Both components of the typical pilot's schizophrenic view of risk are correct: flying is indeed dangerous in the aggregate, but the major sources of danger are largely predictable and controllable. This split awareness of the risks of flying also plays a large part in the way pilots learn to manage fear, or at least that has been the case for me. Learning to fly means going through experiences that are emotionally frightening, even after you have satisfied yourself that rationally there is little or no reason to be alarmed. The same thing is true of learning to swim, learning to drive, learning to ride a bike, but the emotional stakes are naturally higher in becoming comfortable with an airplane. To me the most frightening moments in learning to fly were not the first solo flight, precisely because of the buildup and concentration, but the third or fourth solo outings, as I began wondering how long my lucky streak would last. When aiming straight for the "landing point" on the runway during one of these flights, from perhaps two miles away and 800 feet up, part of my brain would be thinking, "You know, if I mishandle this next minute of my life, I will be dead." With enough landings I stopped thinking that and just concentrated on procedures that I did, in fact, know how to carry out successfully—as everyone does while driving on busy roads, when mishandling even the next three seconds can leave you dead.

The same was true through a variety of other firsts: the first solo "long cross-country," a trip to an airport at least fifty nautical miles from your starting point, which for me meant a trip from the Maryland suburbs of Washington, D.C., to Charlottesville, Virginia. My thoughts en route were, What if I can't handle this far-off airport? What if the engine stops over the mountains? What if I can't find my way back? Rationally I had answers to each of these questions—I'd actually been to the airport before with an instructor; there was virtually no chance that the engine would stop; I knew the procedures for "finding" myself again if I got lost. But that didn't keep me from wondering through the whole flight.

Another frightening "first" was my first solo encounter with "moderate turbulence," which is the official aviation term for what most passengers would describe as extremely bumpy and unpleasant passage through the air. Intellectually I knew this would not shake the plane apart or push it from the sky, but since I hadn't undergone and survived it before I didn't know that viscerally and firsthand. Acquiring experience in airplanes, like experience with driving or boating or bicycling, largely means learning the difference between things that merely seem frightening and those that truly should cause worry and concern. For example, the bumpy air of summer "thermals" gravely alarms many passengers, since the air currents may shoot the plane up or down a hundred feet or more without warning. But the thermals pose no more genuine risk than a bumpy road does to a car. On the other hand, the appearance of a thin, nearly invisible layer of ice on the front of an airplane's wing is a matter of very serious concern, though the passenger might not even notice it, since if the ice gets thick enough the wing will lose its airfoil shape and no longer be able to lift the plane.

Where a pilot wants to place himself on this spectrum of risk determines what kind of flying experience he will have. If he flies only in the daytime, and only when the skies are clear, and only with comfortable reserves of gas, the time he spends in an airplane will be statistically at least as safe as any time he spends driving a car. But in applying those rules he will also preemptively cancel many trips that would in fact have turned out safely, he will not reach destinations to which the airplane could have taken him quickly, and he will miss some of the experience that through the last century has drawn people to flight.

The paying, commercial customer will properly insist on planes that operate near this "zero additional risk" end of the continuum. To be clear, this means small planes that are at least as safe as modern cars, and eventually nearly as safe as airliners. Pilots, who fly more, would have even more reason to welcome these planes as they arrive. But because pilots of small planes view flight both as an efficient means of conveyance and as a source of satisfaction in itself, for them the degree of acceptable risk in flight is higher than it is for civilians who are passengers. Much of the point of today's training and safety programs for pilots is to allow them to feel that the undeniable risks of flight are within the "acceptable" range.

"Acceptable" risk? Even in today's safety-obsessed Western society, people constantly accept increased risk of death as the price of activities they find enjoyable or worthwhile. In 1997, a year in which 667 people died in general aviation crashes, 821 people died in recreational boating accidents in the United States.[4] More than 2,100 people died while riding motorcycles. At least 825 died on bicycles. All would have been safer if they had avoided these activities. Despite their example, millions of people still find boating and cycling worth the risk. On average at least a dozen people drown every day in the United States—more in the summer, at seashores, pools, and lakes. Water is dangerous, but people continue to dive in.

All of these activities attract more people than GA flying does, so their per capita risk is lower. But they serve as reminders that even activities that are dangerous in aggregate can be "rational." Each participant judges whether the risk seems acceptable by a combination of factors: the overall probability of harm, the severity of harm if it occurs, how much of the risk the individual can reduce, and what the offsetting benefit might be.

The Klapmeiers knew that small plane crashes follow strong, predictable patterns, and from observing the patterns they thought that making their plane safer would really mean three things:

- making the plane easier to fly, so as to reduce the number of crashes caused by pilots who are confused, overwhelmed, panicked, lost, or in some other way prone to "pilot error";
- making the plane's own systems more robust and reliable, so there would be fewer crashes due to mechanical error;
- making the plane more crashworthy, so that its passengers had a better chance of surviving the accidents that would inevitably occur.

Cirrus's efforts in the third category, crashworthiness, were eventually the most controversial and notable, since they led to the decision to add a built-in parachute capable of lowering the entire airplane to the ground. But its efforts in the first area—simpler flying—were probably more important, and also more closely in line with what NASA's research had shown about the main cause of small-plane catastrophes.

Pilots are both annoyed and reassured by the typical post-crash investigation that leads to the conclusion that "pilot error" caused the crash. Annoyed because it often doesn't explain much, and is used as a catchall for anything that has gone wrong. But reassured, oddly and perhaps inappropriately, since the calm, twenty-twenty hindsight analysis of a doomed pilot's mistakes allows others to say, "Oh, it's obvious where he went wrong. I would never do that."

In the days of Lindbergh and Earhart, "pilot error" might be said to include climbing into the cockpit in the first place, since the engines were so unreliable and the navigational systems were so crude. Today, even though small planes are still mechanically more fragile than either big airliners or ordinary cars, the airplane itself is the direct cause of accidents in a small minority of cases.[5]

In small planes, most of what goes wrong involves the pilot getting overwhelmed and into trouble. He flies into a thunderstorm, because he didn't have a clear sense of where the bad weather was, and finds that he cannot control the airplane in the violent up- and downdrafts. He's trying to go over a mountain range in the winter, and suddenly he gets into freezing clouds that coat his plane with ice, destroying its ability to fly. He gets lost, and panics, and forgets how to keep the plane flying safely. Or he is a victim of the most common cause of accidents: he has not been trained to fly by instruments alone, but suddenly he finds that he has flown into a cloud bank and can't tell up from down. This, again, has become famous as the John F. Kennedy Jr. scenario.

You might think that pilots would avoid dwelling on such episodes. In fact, pilot training is an immersion in case studies of how pilots went wrong. The goal of the horror stories is to impress on prospective pilots that airplanes are not inherently dangerous, but that the consequences of recklessness or sloppiness are grave. Such an emphasis is all to the good. But the Klapmeier brothers reasoned that the emphasis was excessive. It was like the auto industry's claim in the fifties that "the nut behind the wheel" was the ultimate cause of car crashes, and therefore there was no point in talking about seat belts, or air bags, or innovations that could protect fallible human beings against the mistakes they would inevitably make. And in designing their plane, the Klapmeiers thought the first big step toward safety should be to make its operation as simple as it could realistically be. It should be easy for the pilot to know where he was; easy to figure out where he was going; easy to control the plane.

"What is so hard about flying in the weather?" Alan Klapmeier asks rhetorically. "Actually navigating toward your destination is not hard. The hard part is the *work* you have to do to stay oriented and know what's coming next."

A surprisingly large portion of the effort in flight-training and aircraft design has been devoted to the simplest seeming navigational challenges: helping the pilot know where he is and where he's going. The tools available for answering these questions as of the early nineties, when Cirrus was beginning its design work, were obviously far superior to those of the twenties, when gyroscopes were first introduced. Or those of the early thirties, when pilots followed actual illuminated beacons, which showed a million-candlepower signal every ten seconds, from hilltop to hilltop. Or those of the forties and early fifties, when pilots navigated via "A-N ranges." These were radio beacons that broadcast the Morse code for the letter A, which is "dot-dash," on one side of the proper course to a radio marker, and the Morse code for the letter N, "dash-dot," on the other side. If the plane was heading right toward the station, the A and N signals were equally strong—and the dots and dashes cancelled each other out, so the pilot heard one steady buzzing tone.

Navigation improved significantly by the end of the fifties, when large numbers of new navigational devices known as "VORs" were installed. (The initials stand for Very high frequency Omnidirectional Range.) Whereas the A-N range could offer a binary, "you're to the left" or "you're to the right" indication, the VORs allowed planes to follow an exact bearing to or from a station. For example, you could go due east from the VOR at Los Angeles International Airport, or head toward an destination that was on a 330-degree magnetic heading from O'Hare.

The VORs were effective but far from intuitive. The main reason pilots consider it difficult to earn an instrument rating is not simply the mechanical and psychological training necessary to get used to handling a plane when you can't see the ground. Learning how to make the imaginative leap from the gauges and dials on the instrument panel to a mental picture of where you stand on the map is the larger intellectual challenge.

The limits of these previous navigational systems explain why the advent of Global Positioning System (GPS) navigation, from the seventies onward, had such an impact on aviation. It allowed pilots to do what had been their dream all along—essentially to have a "moving map," or "God's eye" view, of where they are going and how all the relevant factors, of weather, terrain, lightning, other obstacles, and their destination, fit together in one place.

By the midnineties, companies were competing with each other to expand and perfect such displays. NASA promoted the goal of the "all glass cockpit," similar to what had become standard in big airliners. In this cockpit, dozens of small "steam gauge" dials would be replaced with two big computerized displays. On the left would be a "primary flight display," with all the necessary indicators of how the plane was flying (speed, altitude, heading, rate of climb, rate of turn, etc.), presented in intuitive graphic form. This could even work like a video game, graphically representing the "highway in the sky" along which the pilot should fly from takeoff to landing. On the right would be a "multifunction display," showing a range of information relevant to the trip:

nearby storms, nearby mountains, monitoring information from the engines, and so on. One design from Bruce Holmes's team at NASA looked like this (see below), with the "primary flight display" on the left and the "multifunction display" on the right.

Even for small planes, companies had by the nineties come up with indicators designed to give easy visual warning of terrain hazards. For instance, points higher than the plane's current altitudes would show up in red, points safely below in green. Another kind of display (shown on the next page) might indicate to the pilot at a glance where his plane is heading; where its flight plan will take it (shown by a purple line); where nearby lighting strikes might be (yellow crosses); where controlled airspace is (blue outlines); and other information.

Such a display was actually used in the Cirrus, as one of several "moving maps" meant to give the pilot an easy guide at all times

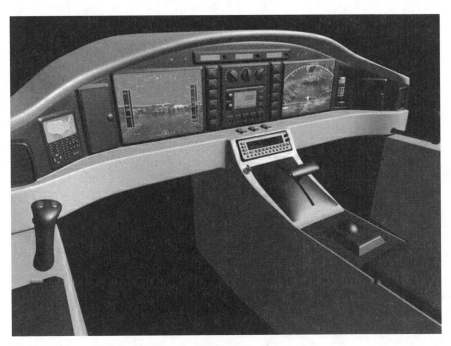

NASA's concept of the small-plane cockpit of the future.

to where he was and which way he was headed. It was a screen twelve inches across, placed in the center of the instrument panel.

"Some of the old macho pilots tell me that they can get all the same info from their gauges, so why do they need to have that picture?" Alan Klapmeier says. "Usually the way I can get to them is to say, 'OK, you don't need any of this—but think how nice it would be for your spouse to know where you were! And of course part of what makes the rear seat passengers feel comfortable is that *they* can see this big moving map too and know where they are. That is a huge factor."

Navigation and "situational awareness" display in the SR20.

In addition to simplified navigation, Cirrus (with NASA's urging) wanted to simplify other aspects of operating the plane as well. Although the Cirrus team did not use this analogy themselves, this was a clear step toward a "Macintosh" rather than "DOS-Windows" model for the airplane. That is, any choice, control, or adjustment that the pilot didn't absolutely have to be involved in, should be concealed as much as possible from the pilot. And many of these traditional choices and controls were taken away from the pilot of a Cirrus airplane.

For instance, the SR20 has "fixed landing gear," wheels that are always extended in the "down" position, rather than retractable wheels that the pilot must remember to put down before landing and pull up when the plane is aloft. Traditionally a "straight leg" plane, with fixed landing gear, meant a slow plane, or a plane suitable mainly for training. For a plane to go fast it had to avoid the drag of those extended wheels.

"It turns out that below 160 knots, 'cleanly faired' landing gear [ones with the right teardrop-shaped aerodynamic housing] are just as good as retractables," Paul Johnston explains. "You lost a couple knots in speed, but you definitely made up for it in avoiding the weight, expense, and complexity of a retractable gear system." Asking yourself for the tenth time before landing, Will *this* be the time I forget to put the wheels down?, is one additional source of stress for a pilot in the most stressful part of a flight. No landing-gear switch means one more thing the pilot can't forget to do.[6]

There were other similar, simplifying changes in the way the Cirrus pilot would control the plane's power, its propeller setting, and the flow of fuel to the engine.[7] The effects were similar to those of the shift from early twentieth century cars, in which the driver had to "advance the magnetos" and start the engine with a crank, to models with automatic transmission. Or the change in skiing, with the advent of progressively shorter and easier-to-control skis. "Think about the change in the computer industry," Alan Klapmeier says. "Thirty years ago 'experts' would say: No one can afford them, no one is smart enough to use them, and no one needs a computer anyway. When I was in college we had a 'computer center.' If you couldn't do FORTRAN, you were kind of looked down on. Then a bunch of people came up with this idea of 'user friendly' and that 'everybody' should be able to work a computer. But there were a bunch of computer people who thought that horrible because it just made things too easy.

"Well, that's what aviation has done. I've had people tell me, at air shows: 'But if you do that, then anybody will be able to fly!' Yeah! That's the idea!"


After streamlining operations for the pilot, the next part of the safety equation was to try to reduce the chance that the plane itself would induce problems. Apart from the obvious elements of mechanical safety—a tested engine, a sturdy airframe—here the main objective was to help the plane resist the "stall-spin" problem that is the source of many airplane accidents.

"Stall" has a meaning in aviation that is specific and important, but that inconveniently is different from the general understanding of the term. After a crash, it is common to read newspaper speculation that the "engine stalled"—this explanation, for instance, was part of the initial reporting on the crash in October 2000 that killed the governor of Missouri, Mel Carnahan, along with his son and associates.

Sometimes airplane engines stop—most often because they run out of gas, occasionally because a cylinder blows up or a crankshaft fails. But they almost never stop because of a "stall" like one that would affect a stick-shift car going up a steep hill. An automotive stall occurs when too great a load is suddenly put on the engine. In airplanes it is the wings that stall, not the engine, and they stall because circumstances no longer permit air to flow over them in a way that can keep the plane up.

The fundamental cause of an airplane stall is that the "angle of attack," the angle at which the wing meets the oncoming air, has become too great.[8] If the angle of attack were zero, the wing would be absolutely level, or horizontal, relative to the wind. If the angle of attack were 90 degrees, the wing would be at right angles to the wind, which would run directly into the wing's underside. When the angle of attack is greater than zero and less than about 18 degrees, the wing produces the lift that holds up the plane. The exact mechanics of its doing so are beside the point, except that they require the wind to flow relatively smoothly over the curved top surface of the wing. The wing can produce lift as long as the wind is following that top surface smoothly. The wing stalls, and stops producing lift, if the angle is too steep and the wind is instead churned into turbulent eddies when it hits the wing. Many things about airflow can be illustrated by water, including this point. If a smooth rock protrudes a small distance above a stream's surface, the water will follow the rock's contours and flow along them swiftly. If the rock is too tall or its edges are too sharp, the water does not go over the top but becomes turbulent whitewater.

Essentially, a wing stalls when the airflow turns into whitewater. Learning to prevent this is the central object of a student pilot's first few lessons. A wing will stall if the plane's speed through the air becomes too slow, or (similar but slightly different) if the wing's angle to the air becomes too steep. Then the plane abruptly stops flying, turning into a falling object like a brick. There are ways to recover from a stall—indeed, students practice doing this dozens of times—but not if it happens too close to the ground.

To make matters worse, when the airflow over a wing is disturbed and the plane stalls instead of flies, not only does the wing stop lifting the plane. It also can no longer help steer the plane. In most cases, a plane turns by using the ailerons to give one wing more lift than the other. That wing goes up, the other goes down, and the plane starts flying in an arc toward a new heading rather than in a straight line. But when there is no smooth air flowing over them, the wings can't steer the plane left or right anymore. This can lead to the spin, which in turn is the beginning of many fatal accidents, as the plane heads to the ground in a corkscrew and the pilot's usual ways of correcting course can make things worse.[9]

In the early eighties, designers at NASA had come up with a plan that they thought could greatly reduce these difficulties, by making the "stall-spin" scenario far less likely. What was particularly dangerous was the quick sequence of a stall, which made the plane fall rather than fly, followed by a spin, which kept the pilot from using the wings to correct his course. The question was how to prevent it, and NASA felt it had found the answer with "wing cuffs."

If you look carefully at the wing of the Cirrus SR20, you notice that something odd happens halfway down the wing's leading edge. There is a distinct gap where the wing's curvature is broken and a new shape begins. It is subtly visible at a distance, and it is obvious close up, (as in the photo below).

This difference is the wing's "cuff." In essence, it lets the plane fly as if it had two different kinds of wings. The inboard part of the wing—the "wing root," closest to the airplane's body—is more steeply angled upward. It therefore has a higher angle of attack, which in turn means that as the plane nears a stalling condition, the inboard part of the wing will show all the warning signs of a stall while the outboard part is still flying. The warning signs of a stall are many. The plane begins to shake. An alarm horn begins to sound, triggered when the airflow across the wing is too slow to

"Wing cuffs," developed by NASA, reduce the risk of stalling the plane.

support flight. In principle pilots could use these warning signs to avert a stall before it really sets in (usually by pointing the plane's nose down)—and while the outer parts of the wing are still "flying" and therefore still provide left-right control.

Planes have for years been designed to accomplish something similar to what the cuffs do. On most planes, the "camber," or upper curvature, of the wing changes as the wing goes from the plane's body out toward the tip, in order to make a stall affect the "wing root" before it affects the wing tip. The idea, again, has been that when a pilot sees that he is nearing a stall, the most important part of the wings—the part near the tip, where the ailerons are, which allows him to steer the plane left or right—will still function. By increasing the difference in angle of attack between the root and tip portions of the wing, the cuffs do this in a much more definite way.

Keeping the pilot oriented, keeping the controls simple, and making the plane as stable as possible were part of the safety approach. There were two more elements. One was to learn from the automobile industry—perhaps a startling concept, but one that recurs throughout the airplane process—to make the body of planes more survivable. When Ralph Nader wrote *Unsafe at Any Speed* in the midsixties, the typical automobile interior was full of sharp edges and projections that proved lethal in collisions. A head-on crash, in that era before seat belts, air bags, or collapsing steering wheels, often left a driver impaled on the steering column. Since the sixties, cars have acquired dozens of features that collectively make them more crashworthy. With many more miles being driven than in the sixties, and despite more drivers behaving more aggressively, the total death toll from traffic accidents is significantly down.

Many similar innovations went into the SR20: Four-point seatbelts, with the same effect as a shoulder harness. A different kind of frame, to absorb energy and make crashes more survivable. Even this was part of a NASA project, to see how when the plane nosed into a bank of trees or a wall the shock could be directed away from the passengers, as with a modern car.

And there was one other innovation, the most noticeable single safety feature and the one that caused the most bickering and sneering from the rest of the business. That was equipping the SR20 with a parachute for the entire plane.

On May 2, 1984, when Alan Klapmeier was twenty-five years old, he was taking a flying lesson at the Sauk-Prairie airport, just north of Madison, Wisconsin. It was late afternoon, and the sun was low in the sky. Klapmeier was in the pilot's seat, with an instructor sitting next to him. He had just taken off and was turning away from the airport, with the sun at his back. A plane was nearing the airport from the opposite direction, flying with the sun in the pilot's face. The other pilot was a friend of Klapmeier's who had taken off from a tiny turf strip called Lodi Lakeland ten miles away. He was flying a variant of the Piper Cub called the PA-7, and he had no radio installed. Pilots may fly "NRDO," or "no radio," as long as they stay out of certain kinds of controlled airspace.

Every person who learns to fly is amazed by the reality of the "big sky"—you may fly for hours across several states and not see another plane, except around airports. Most midair collisions therefore happen within five miles of an airport, and most happen in good weather, since on bad-weather days, the planes are flying on instrument flight plans and are being separated by a controller's instructions.

On this clear spring day, near an airport, Klapmeier's plane collided with the other one. The first either knew of the other's existence was the instant the planes hit. The wing of Klapmeier's plane sliced through the strut that supported the other plane's wing. That plane lost its ability to fly and spun into the ground, killing the pilot.

Klapmeier's plane had lost part of its right wing in the impact. The plane could still fly, but Klapmeier had to ram the control yoke hard to the left to keep the plane flying straight. After the collision Klapmeier instinctively pulled back on the throttle to reduce power, but the instructor pushed it back in. When a plane's control surfaces are damaged, it needs more airspeed to maintain control. Klapmeier steered the plane back toward the runway, shoving the yoke to the left the whole time. As he neared a landing, Klapmeier realized that he had pushed the yoke as far left as it would go. As he remembers them, each of the next few seconds contained its own complete drama. Act 1: the yoke reached its "stop" and would go no farther. Act 2: the plane began rolling over to the right. Act 3: the plane rolled so far that its wing struck the ground, sending the craft into a cartwheeling crash. But no—act 3 never happened, because at the end of act 2, with a second or so to spare, Klapmeier felt the wheels touch the runway.

"They were very, very lucky that they survived," Dale Klapmeier says of his brother and the instructor. From such an episode some people might have drawn the conclusion that flying was too great a risk to expose oneself to again. Alan Klapmeier drew the conclusion that small planes were too risky and had to be made safer. "This obviously was an important part of our decision that planes had to be made a lot safer, in many ways," Alan says. All the preliminary steps in designing the SR20 were important parts of improving its safety—the "situational awareness" and visibility, the crashworthiness, and the rest. But he began a search to bring to small airplanes the last-ditch safety measure the military had long applied, for circumstances in which mechanical failures, reckless judgments, or simple bad luck put the pilot in an impossible situation. The military did so with its ejection seats. When a pilot used them, it meant that the plane would be lost, and the pilot could still be injured, but it was an alternative to near-certain death if he stayed with the plane.

Ejection seats were not practical for small planes—they were too heavy and expensive and would not work with planes that had solid roofs, rather than canopies to blow off. Nor did it make sense to equip every passenger in a cramped small plane with a back-parachute, like early air mail pilots used to wear. Among other reasons, the doors on small planes are not made for fast or easy escape, especially from the back. But since the sixties certain "ultralight" planes—the inexpensive homebuilt craft that satisfied many people's desire to fly but crashed with alarming frequency— had been equipped with rescue parachutes for the plane as a whole. The Klapmeiers decided that this is what their new airplane would have to have as well. From the start it was built with the idea that a whole-airplane parachute would come as standard equipment—not an extra-price option, not something that could be either selected or disabled later on, but an integral part of the plane, like the energy-absorbing bumpers in modern cars.

"It kind of goes against the pilot culture to admit that people are going to make mistakes," Alan Klapmeier told me the first time I met him. In fact, the aviation literature is full of discussion about why pilots made the mistakes that led to fatal crashes, so as to emphasize to still-living pilots that they should be extra careful, take the extra training, be aware that carelessness can have terrible results.

These messages are all good, but Klapmeier was saying that they weren't the most effective way actually to increase the number of people who survived the small-plane system. "I don't know about you, but when I'm flying I'm thinking about my kids, or thinking about my work, or thinking about the next thing I have to do—rather than thinking every minute about the next thing that's going to happen in the air," he said. "The emphasis on non-stop pilot training will work for the air force and the airlines. Professional pilots know that their job is flying, and they stay focused on it the entire time. But it won't do for the unprofessional—let's say the 'nonprofessional' pilot, the pilot who is flying for personal transportation. He's not likely to have the same focus." Rather than fatalism about the consequences if a pilot makes an error—or, with no particular error, runs into misfortune—the idea was to limit the consequences so they could live to learn better. That, after all, was the military way.

"If we had known exactly how hard this was going to be, we wouldn't have done it," Paul Johnston said roughly a decade after the initial decision to build a plane with a parachute inside. "We probably would have said: OK, let's pursue this as a goal, but in the meantime, let's get the first plane out the door. It's not that we would never have done it, but if we'd known from the start that it would take two years and all this development work.... So it was probably a good thing that we made the leap and decided to do it, so we had to keep moving forward and get it done."

The conceptual problem with a whole-airplane parachute is that no one had made it work in quite this way before. The Cirrus airplane would be four or five times heavier than the typical ultra-light, and it would be going much faster when the parachute needed to arrest a fall. The parachute would therefore have to be much bigger and stronger—and would have to be the result of another series of elaborate trade-offs. There would have to be no chance of its going off unintentionally, at the wrong moment. On takeoff or landing, times when the airplane was close to the ground and close to its own stalling speed, the sudden deployment of a parachute could be disastrous. And there would have to be no chance of the chute's failing when the pilot pulled the handle as his last chance for survival. Here the record was good: since the early eighties, parachutes from the Ballistics Recovery Systems company, or BRS, of St. Paul, Minnesota, had saved more than a hundred lives in ultralight crashes, without any unintentional deployments or apparent failures to deploy.[10]

The straps that would support the Cirrus's parachute would be embedded in the fuselage of the plane. They would reside beneath a thin covering layer of fiberglass that would keep them invisible and secure through the normal life of the airplane—but then would have to rip off instantly if the chute were ever deployed. The parachute itself would have to be strong enough to stop the descent of an object weighing one and a half tons and diving toward the ground at well over one hundred miles an hour, but its deployment would have to be gradual enough that it did not rip the plane's structure apart in the process of saving it. "The problem to solve with the chute was how to open it fast enough that it will be safe and effective, but slow enough not to overload the plane" was the way Alan Klapmeier put it.

From late 1994 through late 1996, trying to figure out the parachute was the preoccupation of half a dozen members of the Cirrus team. Four were the central participants: Paul Johnston and Pat Waddick as the designers, and Scott Anderson and Gary Black as the pilots. Black, a former navy pilot, was in his early forties; the others were in their thirties. They started through the sequence of problems to be solved to make a usable small-plane parachute. How would it deploy? The BRS company had solved that, with a rocket pack that shot the parachute off the back of planes. This is the one that had worked reliably in the ultralight crashes. What if the plane were upside down or spinning? The rocket pack shot the parachute a safe distance behind the plane in either case. What if the plane were in a high-speed dive? The goal was a deployment system that would arrest the descent with a loss of only 1,000 feet of altitude, so if the pilot pulled it in what would otherwise be the last few seconds before impact, he could still be saved.

"What made this so hard?" Paul Johnston says. "The speeds were greater than any other installation, in the ultralights. Our low-wing structure meant there was no place to attach the parachute to a wing spar. The whole dynamics of placing it were a big unknown. This had to be the largest parachute ever made of this lightweight material, Kevlar and other lightweight materials. Developing the rocket, developing the test plane, figuring out how to bury the straps on the fuselage so they would stay in permanently but rip out easily—that was complicated too. And then you have to test this thing. It has to handle 20,000 pounds of load in a very sudden manner, and it cannot fail. All those things combined made us have lots of chute failures in the beginning. We were approaching forty test drops before we got something good and consistent.

"And there was no history. You couldn't go find out what the person did before you. It took a good two years of hard work, and that was not planned in at the beginning."

The main problems involved "scaling up" the system to handle the weight of a four-person plane. The testing team spent weeks in the high desert of Southern California. Because they had no actual Cirrus plane yet to use for tests, they would fill 55-gallon drums with sand, until they had enough for a test pallet weighing 3,625 pounds—700 pounds above the projected maximum gross weight of the plane. They would load these pallets into the back of a C-123 cargo plane, shove them out the back, let them free-fall until they reached nearly 200 miles an hour, and then push a switch to deploy the chutes. They would film the results on the way down.

"We drilled *a lot* of holes in the desert in those days," Paul Johnston says. "We put a lot of sand back in."

The crucial idea came originally from BRS. The trick in engineering is not always making things that work quickly; it can be harder to make things that are *slow*. And as a way of slowing the deployment of the chute, so that its shock force was spread over several seconds rather than hitting all at once, Johnston and others applied BRS's concept of a "slider ring." This was a device that encircled the lines leading from the parachute canopy to the plane. When the chute first deployed and the plane's speed through the air was at its greatest, wind force on the ring itself would keep it near the top of the lines, where it would allow the chute to open only part way.

How the parachute for the SR20 is supposed to work.

Over the next few seconds, as the drag from the partly opened chute began to slow the plane, the slider ring would move farther down the shroud lines—allowing the chute to open more fully, which would slow the plane more, which would let the ring move farther down until within a few seconds the chute was fully deployed.

When the drops out of the tankers proved that the ring would work, the team was by 1997 ready for its first tests with an actual SR20 fuselage. This required an adjustment of its own. The parachute was designed to save the lives of the people in the plane, but not to spare the plane itself from damage. "The airplane is designed to absorb energy on impact, and it does so by sacrificing itself," Johnston says. By this time, the total supply of Cirrus airplanes was two. In order to test the chute repeatedly, the team

How the parachute began deploying in a test flight.

needed to deploy the parachute, have it stop the plane and lower it into a descent—and then permit the pilot to start the engine in the air and cut the chute loose as the plane neared the ground, so that it could land normally to be tested again. "We needed a system that would instantly release the chute at its three attachment points, just with a pull on a little handle—but just previous to that, the attach points would have had to hold 20,000 pounds of tugging load. Making sure that worked was our biggest risk going into the testing" Johnston says.

Because the desert air gets hot and bumpy as the day goes on, the team would get up at 4 A.M. and rehearse each morning's drop. At dawn the main test pilot, Scott Anderson, would fly the test plane, white with high-visibility orange marking points on the tips of its wings, tail, and elevators, to make its motions easier

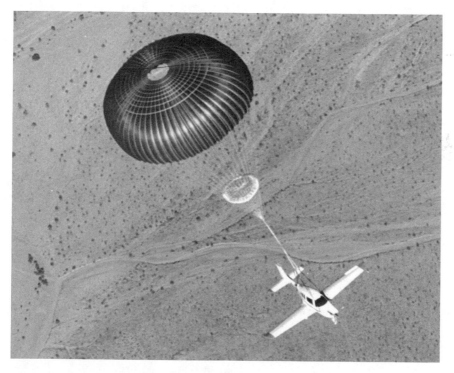

Drifting toward earth after complete deployment.

to identify on film. Chase planes, helicopters, occasionally a jet would accompany Anderson, to film the test from every angle. Eight times, spaced over twelve weeks, Anderson shot off the parachute from a variety of simulated in-flight problems. Dives and spins, to simulate recoveries after a midair collision, or after a pilot became disoriented in the clouds. Deployments from level flight, to approximate the consequences of an engine failure. Before the FAA will certify a plane, the manufacturers must show that a pilot can bring the plane out of a spin that has developed. The SR20 met this standard through a combination of spin-resistance—the cuffed wings making it hard for a spin to start—and the parachute that would arrest the fall before the plane had lost 1,000 feet of altitude.

Cameramen took photos of the plane falling, being arrested by the chute, and then taking off on its own power as it neared the ground. Sometimes the shrouds connecting the chute to the plane would not all cut away cleanly at the end of the test, and Anderson's plane would be left hanging dangerously by one wing or in a nose-down position. Each time he managed to free the plane and fly away safely; otherwise, he would have had to jump out and descend with an individual parachute on his back.

By early 1998, the company was satisfied that it had a product that not only would meet the FAA's explicit safety standards but could also and more broadly provide a measure of safety that was not there before. If an engine failed at night, or over the mountains; if the plane ran into another plane and lost a wing; if the pilot suffered a heart attack or passed out at the controls; if a pilot without an instrument rating found himself in the middle of fog or clouds; if a pilot with an instrument rating encountered a sudden power failure or other emergency that made all the dials and gauges go dead—in these and any other in extremis situations, there would be one more option, which would be to pull the handle and deploy the chute. The analogy, again, would be to a military pilot bailing out of his fighter plane, with the significant differences that the plane would not career off at high speed with the risk of destroying something on the ground, and that all occupants of the plane would be protected at once, rather than having chutes that deployed individually.

Various aspects of the SR20 fell short of its designers' and customers' aspirations. It was not quite as fast or light as everyone had hoped, and not as cheap as initially planned. The subcontractor making its guidance screens didn't adopt and apply new technology as quickly as it might, so that Cirrus was considering another supplier two years after the plane went on the market. These were imperfections; but the only aspect of the plane's design to provoke open hostility was the inclusion of a parachute. The reaction was like that of motorcyclists told for the first time that they had to wear helmets. There was one rational level of objection—that the parachute and rocket added eighty pounds to the weight of the plane, or nearly 10 percent of its entire useful load. Alan Klapmeier liked to ask, in response, how much the second engine in a twin-engine plane weighed. The answer was many hundreds of pounds, but many people found this a perfectly reasonable investment in safety and reliability—even though running a second engine nearly doubled the plane's overall operating and maintenance costs. Why all the fuss about eighty pounds?

The answer involved the second, not-quite-rational, level of resistance, which grew from deeper feelings about the untrammeled independence that pilots should enjoy, and their resentment of anything that smacked of the nanny-state.

Pilots began raising doubts on their computerized bulletin boards and in discussions at conventions. Maybe the parachute could actually create more problems than it solved if it gave pilots a false sense of security about getting into situations they might not know how to get out of. Maybe the parachute descent itself could prove hazardous—once the rocket deploying the chute went off, the pilot had no further control over where the plane would end up. It would drift horizontally with the wind, and descend at a rate equivalent to a ten-foot straight drop, which could be a nasty jolt at the end. What if it blew onto the rocks? What if a plane came down on a lake or ocean, and the chute draped across the cabin on the water's surface and trapped occupants inside as the airplane sank? Pilots train time and again to land a plane with minimal damage, even if the engine has gone out. Wouldn't that be a better option in many "emergency" situations, rather than letting a panicky pilot go for the chute?[11] What if an engine failed on takeoff—the most dangerous time for a mechanical failure, since the plane is too close to the ground to pick a good landing spot and glide there? Wouldn't the chute be useless at best in that circumstance? Since a parachute is not a perfect solution, why not let each pilot decide for himself whether he needs a crutch like this in order to feel safe aloft?

The Cirrus representatives eventually developed what politicians or marketers might think of as targeted responses to the queries. To pilots who raised these complaints, they consistently said: Good point! The parachute could be risky. If other options are there, then use them. But when there are *no options left*, and a pilot faces a situation that without a parachute would very likely mean death, then having the parachute is a lot better than not. And by definition such circumstances exist; otherwise, planes would never crash.

"Usually when people are resisting the parachute, there's an argument where they *finally* agree," Alan Klapmeier says. "I'll say, OK, I know that you're such a great pilot that you can always land the plane safely. But what if you have a heart attack? And they'll say, 'When it's my time, it's my time.' And I'll ask: What about your beloved wife and children who are traveling along with you? Don't you care about them? One guy actually said, 'Well, they should know if they're with me that when it's my time, it's their time too.' But most of them stop arguing at that point."

"You've still got all the standard pooh-poohing," Paul Johnston says. "The other companies' websites will say, 'Well, we feel it's better to concentrate on preventing accidents than saving you from accidents.'" Johnston continues, "And that's a very good thing to say and do. We all should prevent accidents. But, as we all know, they still happen.

"Then you get the standard comment: Well, *I* would never pull one. In reality, when I started off on this program—which was Alan's idea—I thought, Would I really pull it? Is it worth the weight? I had a skeptical eye to this whole thing. I didn't change my mind until we did the full deployments and saw that it performed better than expected. The loads were lower. The loss of altitude in recovery was shorter. In level flights we were recovering in 250 to 350 feet. In spin recovery, we were hoping to come in with less than 1,200 feet of loss, and we came in under 900. After seeing the results, we looked at our fleet of test planes and said: Let's get that chute on all our test planes! We retrofitted it to our other planes, though it was not that easy to do after they'd already been built."

Still, when explaining the origin and function of the parachute to a crowd of several hundred pilots, at the world's premiere, hard-core piloting event, the Oshkosh AirVenture in the summer of 2000, Johnston stuck to the "just another option" line. "The operating handbook says, this is for use in *life-threatening emergencies*. When should you pull the handle? You should pull it when you think it would help."

That's the careful argument for the pilots. For everyone else, the only question to answer was: *What took so long???*

"There is no question that this is a psychological advantage," Ian Bentley, a sales executive of Cirrus, says. "It's a very easy-to-understand safety device. Everybody can learn how to use the parachute in ten seconds. If the guy next to you croaks, you've got a way out. That is a great psychological relief for many people."

A discussion board among potential Cirrus owners was full of comments about how the pilot himself might claim not to care about the parachute but it certainly was reassuring to the civilians coming along for the ride. "The parachute does a lot for nonfliers," one typical posting said. "It isn't a big issue for me, but my wife really likes the idea and several friends who won't fly because of their (or their wife's) fears have indicated that they will fly in the new plane."

"Yeah, there are people who don't like the idea, who can fly their way out of any problem," a Cirrus official said. "But my wife who wouldn't fly before because she was afraid of the way her husband flew the airplane, she now has a way out. Even if we never use the parachute, the knowledge that it's there is a plus to her every time we fly."


By the springtime of 1999, all the efforts seemed to be coming together and paying off for the team at Cirrus. The design choices, the parachute tests, the next electronic displays, the engine testing, the interim financing—for the moment, all of them were taken care of. At aviation shows since 1994, the company had been displaying prototype fuselages of the plane, and taking orders. The price was set at under $150,000; the deposit was a refundable $15,000. By 1995, there were fifty people on the waiting list. By 1996, there were one hundred. In 1997, the company

moved to a new factory in Duluth, where it hoped to begin production. And early in 1998, the most important step of all: application for the "type certificate" from the Federal Aviation
Administration, which would let the SR20 go on sale as a real,
production aircraft and not some kit that people had to build
themselves.

By the late summer of 1998, Cirrus got word through the FAA
that it had met the standards. And at the annual AOPA Expo that
October—the convention of the Aircraft Owners and Pilots Association, the lobby on behalf of small-plane pilots and small airports—Cirrus and Lancair were both awarded the first type
certificates for genuinely new small planes in a generation.

Through the winter of 1998 and early 1999, Dale Klapmeier
concentrated on developing the production line while Alan
worked, as usual, on finance and sales. They continued to hire;
they planned for planes beyond the SR20. The waiting list grew to
more than 300 depositors, who had to put down their $15,000 on
a nonrefundable basis. The first customer on the waiting list grew
increasingly eager to get his plane. This was Walt Conley, a
recently retired corporate executive from Minnesota who had
been raised in the world of flying—he grew up in Hawaii, where
his father was the PanAm manager—and had owned a series of
planes. Even though the SR20 had been fully certified, tests continued to refine the design. And on March 23 came the worst
news in the fifteen years since the brothers had decided to try to
build airplanes together. The very first model off the assembly, an
SR20 with serial number 1001, had crashed. And Scott Anderson,
the test pilot who had endured all the experimental drops with
the parachute, was dead.

# What Makes an Airplane Fly

All pilots accept certain risks, and test pilots accept larger ones. Most pilots are taught to fly the plane within the proven limits of its "performance envelope." Test pilots discover what those limits are. Like policemen, like firemen, like miners or open-sea fishermen, test pilots all know colleagues who have been killed on the job.

Before Scott Anderson, one other person had died during Cirrus's history of flight-testing. In the spring of 1996, a former Space Shuttle astronaut and marine fighter pilot named Robert Overmyer died during a test flight of the futuristic-looking VK-30 that Cirrus was developing. Overmyer had been putting the plane through stall drills when it went into a spin from which he could not recover, and although he was wearing a parachute he did not undo his seat belt or get out of the plane before it crashed. Overmyer, who was in his late fifties, had also been a test pilot for early SR20 prototypes. A large portrait of him in his Space Shuttle flight suit went up in the main reception area of Cirrus's headquarters in Duluth.

But the effect of Anderson's death was more devastating, for a variety of reasons, and for a while it looked as if one crash would mean the end not just of his life but also of the several hundred ambitions that had by that time concentrated in the Cirrus Design Corporation.

Anderson was thirty-three years old at the time of his death, though with his bald head, he could look a decade older. (This photo shows a relatively youthful-looking Anderson next to the plane used for the parachute-drop tests.[1])

Anderson had grown up in Duluth and, typical for people in the business, had "always" wanted to fly. He was the captain of the football team and a star student in high school, and went off to Stanford for college. He came back home and trained for the one job he was convinced he wanted: a slot in the Air National Guard based at Duluth's air base. The guard offered pilots an attractive deal: it trained them to fly a particular airplane, in Anderson's case the F-16 Falcon fighter, and guaranteed that they could serve their flying career based in their hometown, rather than being transferred every few years like regular air force pilots.

Scott Anderson, Cirrus test pilot.

At Stanford, Anderson had received degrees in both history and mechanical engineering, and in Duluth he filled the role of pilots from an earlier, more romantic age, who combined artistic with mechanical interests. In his midtwenties he published a non-fiction book called *Distant Fires*, about a three-month canoe trip that he and a friend had made from Lake Superior to Hudson Bay, retracing a route that Eric Sevareid had written about fifty years earlier, in *Canoeing with the Cree*. Anderson's book was well received and won an American Library Association "best book for young people" award. Later he published a roman à clef called *Unknown Rider*, about the process of training to become a fighter pilot. In Duluth he was a popular, prominent, young-man-with-a-future figure. The Air National Guard operations in Duluth were just across the runway from Cirrus's new factory, and Anderson began working informally with the company in the mid-nineties. He was flying the "chase plane" to observer Robert Overmyer's test during the flight that led to Overmyer's death. Eventually he was hired as Cirrus's director of flight operations. His force of personality made him one of the central figures in the company. In the summer of 1998 he married Laurie De Roche, another Duluth native and flying enthusiast. Anderson proposed as they flew over the Yukon in a small plane, and their wedding reception was at the Park Point Airport, on a sandspit extending from Duluth into Lake Superior. Laurie learned that she was pregnant in early March 1999.

The lore of airplane accidents is that they usually involve a compounding sequence of misfortunes, any one of which, if avoided, would have prevented the entire accident from occurring. This seems to have been the case on March 23, 1999.

The winds around Duluth that morning were extremely gusty. At the time of his flight, they were reported as twenty-eight knots, gusting to thirty-five. Sudden changes in the wind's force or direction put unusual stress on a plane's structure. This is why, when flying through turbulence, pilots are instructed to keep the plane below its "maneuvering speed," the speed at which sudden stress won't expose it to intolerable loads. Anderson was testing the way the plane handled stalls and quick, dramatic maneuvers—going suddenly from a steep left-hand turn to a steep right-hand turn, for instance, or other changes that would be more part of stunt flying than a normal cruise. He was a confident enough pilot that he was known to take a very aggressive hand in moving the controls vigorously up, down, right, left, to see what the plane could take. And even though he had flown the test flights in which Cirrus had developed its parachute, the plane he flew that morning was not yet equipped with a parachute, simply because the production models of the parachutes were still so new that none had yet been fitted to the planes.

The night before, Anderson had called Gary Black, the veteran navy flyer who had joined Cirrus's flight-test squad, to ask him to take the early-morning flight shift. Anderson said he wanted to sleep in; actually he went out for a 6 A.M. swim. Black took the plane up soon after dawn, but found that the winds were too rough for the stall testing he had planned to do. Black passed the keys to Anderson, for a second shift of test-flying, and then left to go with Alan Klapmeier to Chicago in another plane.

A few minutes after he had taken off, Anderson was radioing the tower that he was having trouble with the plane. He made one attempt to land but couldn't control the plane's direction, so he banked away to try again. He made another attempt—but at low altitude he could not control the bank or direction of the plane. It slammed into former air force base buildings adjoining the airport, which after the base's closure had been converted to the Duluth Federal Prison Camp.

Paul Johnston saw the crash out his window and was there

before the ambulance arrived. Over the previous three years he had spent much of his time working on crashworthy structures and seats for airplanes. This required him to study what happened to a plane and its occupants when they came to a near-instantaneous stop. One scenario he had learned to identify, with horror, was the "nose-low impact onto a hard surface." When a plane hits at high speed, nose pointed down, the tail structure is damaged in a distinctive way because of the whiplash effect. When the tail shows that kind of deformation, it means that the plane's occupants have suffered a deceleration of more than one hundred Gs, far more than they could survive.

"Arriving at the scene of the accident, my heart stops as I see the tail damage that indicates a severed tail slap down," Johnston says. It was the sign of the nose-low high-speed impact. "I can only pray that somehow this sign does not foretell the future."

In fact, Anderson was still conscious as he went into the ambulance, and said, "I think I broke my pelvis." He was rushed into the operating room, and the hospital soon filled with friends, colleagues from Cirrus. Relatives, including Laurie Anderson, arrived, and after an hour a doctor emerged to tell her, "It doesn't look good."

"I thought he meant, 'It doesn't look good for his flying F-16s any more," she said a year and a half later. "I'd heard that he'd been talking at the scene." In fact, Anderson was about to die from internal injuries and loss of blood. After he was dead, his parents and widow and friends stood around his bed and held hands. Anderson's father asked them each to speak about what Scott had meant in their lives.

Everyone involved with the company describes the next month as a period of paralysis and shock. Duluth's churches overflowed with crowds for the memorial services. For the company there was the unpleasant coexistence of the loss of a central figure and the practical concern about what this would mean to the firm. "The worst part, obviously, was just the loss of Scott and the emotional effect inside the company," Alan Klapmeier said a year after the event. "He was one of these guys who was just so well liked. Obviously even if he'd been somebody that nobody liked, it would still have been terrible for the company. But when you add to it that everybody felt like they'd lost a close friend—there was this month-long period of shock. Nobody could be effective at doing anything, raising money, working on design, getting the plane into production."

But everyone in the entire business was aware of the awkward balance between grieving for test pilots who died, and trying dispassionately to figure out what exactly had gone wrong and whether it could be fixed quickly. The test pilots devised ways to distance themselves from the impact. Three years earlier, after watching Robert Overmyer go down from his immediate vantage point in the chase plane, Anderson had gone home and watched *The Right Stuff* on his VCR. Gary Black, who had flown the plane just before Anderson, and who would be the first person again to fly a Cirrus after the crash, later said, "You look at it analytically to find out what went wrong. If you know what it is, you fix it. If you don't, you keep looking."[2]

Cirrus survived this as a business mainly because of the behavior and actions of two groups of people. One was the investigative and regulatory group from the relevant federal agencies—the National Transportation Safety Board, which investigates accidents, and the Federal Aviation Administration, which had recently certified the SR20 as safe for sale and use. The NTSB was able to determine within days what had caused the crash—which allowed the FAA not to change its certification or approval for deliveries of the plane. From analyzing radar readings of the path of Anderson's plane, it became obvious that he was having trouble controlling its "roll"—the left-right steering, determined by the ailerons. The engineers soon determined that in a particular set of circumstances, unlikely to occur in normal flight, the ailerons could become jammed. This would happen if the wings were deflected fully upward, as in a violent updraft of wind, at just the moment the pilot was banking the plane severely to one side. Apparently this happened to Anderson, and when it did he could not bring the plane out of a bank.[3] The wings were adjusted to allow a few more millimeters' clearance between the aileron and the wing to eliminate the chance that they could bind. The NTSB lifted a huge cloud from Cirrus by indicating, early, that the likely cause of the accident had been found and corrected. The FAA saw no reason to revoke its certification of the plane nor its decision that deliveries could proceed.

The other group that played a role was Anderson's family. Laurie Anderson was obviously devastated, but she felt no wrath toward the company or the airplane. "My husband believed in the company totally," she said—to the press, to Cirrus employees, to friends in Duluth. "His heart and soul had gone into this company," she said. "Our heart and soul had gone into it. It would all be for nothing if the whole effort died along with him." Over the passing months, after her baby was born and the daily reality of her husband's absence sank in, relations between Laurie Anderson and the team at Cirrus naturally grew more strained. They were moving on to new successes. She was on her own. But she still said that the company owed it to her husband's memory to make the plane a success.

Every organization involved in building flying machines worries about the "Hindenburg scenario." They fear a disaster that, in addition to costing human lives, so permanently damages the reputation of their company, its products, or its technology that they never recover.[4]

Scott Anderson's death, in a brand new plane about to go to the company's very first customer, could have been that event for Cirrus but wasn't. Instead, over the next two years the company struggled with the slower, more familiar form of chronic disaster for start-ups, especially those in aviation. This was the ceaseless effort to raise enough money to give the business a chance for success.

There is a hoary joke in aviation circles about what exactly makes a plane fly. Is it mainly the rapid flow of air across the top of a wing? Or the pressure of air on the bottom? Or mainly the thrust from the engine? The punch line, of course, is that's none of these things. What makes a plane fly is money.

For people who own airplanes, this adage means roughly what the comparable versions would to people who own boats or vacation homes. But it means something more specific and consequential for those who enter the business of building and selling airplanes. Through the eighties and nineties, the classic American story of bright young entrepreneurs achieving start-up success involved people who designed a new kind of software or an Internet site. One reason these "new economy" ventures were so appealing as start-ups is that their initial capital requirements could be so low. Buy a few computers, rent some office space with furniture, pay the salaries of programmers and marketers, and you can have a company. The "lean years" can be that initial six to twelve months while you design the site or program and debug it, but after that it's at least theoretically possible to start recouping costs.

Airplane builders operate at the other end of the capital-requirement chart. Like software or Net sites, they too start with a new idea. But before the idea can be turned into revenue of any sort, the company must survive a long, slow, extremely expensive process. The idea of the plane must be converted into a metal or fiberglass reality. That must be flown and tested to be sure that it's safe. Prototypes are often built and then destroyed, to see how they would stand up to extreme strains in flight or in a crash. All this is before the government gives its blessing to the plane, and after that comes the long process of building a factory, buying machine tools, hiring and training a workforce, and finally, many years after the occurrence of the first idea, getting products into the hands of customers who will pay.

In these circumstances it is hardly surprising that the aircraft industry, like other businesses with big, complex, costly, capital-intensive products, has become more and more concentrated with the passing years. In the twenties more than 150 companies around the world were trying to enter the airplane business. Now there are only two serious contenders in the big-airplane market, Boeing and Airbus, and the list of companies making planes of any size continues to shrink. Thus to imagine success as an airplane-company start-up is similar to dreaming of competing with Ford or Toyota in the automotive business.

This was the trend that the Klapmeier brothers believed they could buck. In other industries, similarly ambitious young people with similarly clear ideas about revolutionary new products had been able to create empires for themselves. The Klapmeiers went into business only a few years after Microsoft and Apple did, and a few years before AOL. But they needed more money to make their dream come true. And the struggle to raise money, which is the hard part of any activity, is the one part of his company's saga that Alan Klapmeier, the money raiser, truly broods about. When talking about the implications of new kinds of airplanes for travel, for convenience, for new applications of technology, he can sound committed but somewhat formulaic, like a politician explaining his school-voucher plan for the two hundredth time. But when he talks about raising money, he seems to be fighting the urge to stride across the room and grab the listener by the lapels. "The hardest part of this project, by far, has been raising the money to do it," he told me more than once, as if the experience had been so grueling that it could barely be conveyed to outsiders. "I know the technology's not a problem. I don't believe the market is a problem. But trying to raise the money is just so … hard, and irrational."

Karl Marx said that capitalists exploit labor; John Kenneth Galbraith once wrote that entrepreneurs, whether they be shopkeepers, inventors, or farmers, necessarily exploit themselves.[5] They subsidize their own risks precisely because established institutions are not willing to take a chance on them.

So it was as the Klapmeiers got going. The working capital through the company's early years, and whenever they encountered a subsequent rough spot, had come from their own family. Having invested more than $3 million by 1990, when the brothers began work on the SR20 in earnest, the family had put in a total of perhaps $15 million by 2000, as the SR20 went into large-scale production. That was less than one-fifth of the $85 million the company had raised by that time, but it was a very substantial share of all the assets the family had.

"Here's what I've learned is an important financing principle," Alan Klapmeier told me, almost every time I talked with him. "If you don't need the money, somebody will give it to you." He had first learned this lesson when watching his parents negotiate the sale of their nursing homes. A hospital chain had approached his father offering to buy the homes. The elder Klapmeiers said thanks for the offer, but their the family business was not for sale.

"The company came back and said, 'No, really, these are the ones we want,'" Alan Klapmeier says. "They kind of ratcheted it up to the point where my parents said, 'OK, if that's what you'll pay, then we will sell.'" Thus did the family generate working capital.

In the fifteen years from the brothers' founding of Cirrus Design, in 1986, to its delivery of its second kind of airplane, the SR22, in 2001, they always needed money. Therefore, true to the corollary of Alan's lesson, they always had trouble raising it. Through the late eighties, when the brothers were trying to develop their kit-plane business, they survived by living on the family farm and converting a barn into their office and production site. "Obviously we were extremely lucky at the early stage that our family believed in us," Alan Klapmeier says. "Dale and I had this vision that investing in general aviation made sense, that we understood the customer, that we could come up with a design that worked. If we had had to go first to investors, there is zero possibility that we could have gotten started. There is just no way we would have found someone else to believe it the way our parents did when we said, We think this plan will work."

The Israviation contract seemed to be a breakthrough, and, at $3 million a year for three years in the early nineties, it was their main income. But it gave them no real breathing room. In the early nineties Cirrus also received three smaller research contracts from NASA, which it expected to add at least several hundred thousand dollars a year to its cash flow. More, but not enough.

Alan Klapmeier says, "I remember lots of times when we'd realize, OK, it's going to take a little more money than we thought. I guess we have to go back to the family meeting and have another discussion. Does this still make sense? Fortunately Mom and Dad would walk through it and say, 'Well, do you still think it's going to be profitable in the future? And why do you think that?' It was the complete opposite of what we got used to with investment bankers later on. Our parents were saying, Show us how this will make sense in the long run. If you can convince us of that, we're convinced."

If they were serious about making real airplanes, they would need to build or move to a real factory. And they would need real money too—more than their parents could provide, even if the parents were willing to put all their assets into the business. So in the early nineties the twenty people who made up the Cirrus Design Corporation juggled several projects: completing the prototype for Israviation, working out plans for the SR20, finding a new home for the factory, and looking constantly for new money.

For the new factory site, they had a bias toward the Midwest. It was their home region. "We like the cold. We like the snow. We like the work ethic," Alan Klapmeier says. Also, with its flatlands, the Midwest is aviator heaven. It is dotted with more airports, closer together, than either the mountainous West or overbuilt East coasts.

They wanted an area with a skilled workforce but not an overheated economy and the tight labor market it would bring. They wanted a smallish city but if possible one with a university, to help attract recruits from elsewhere in the country. Of course the factory would have to be built at or near an airport, and they had a particular kind of airport in mind. It should have big, long runways, and a control tower, and full safety equipment, but not the nonstop air traffic of a busy urban hub. That meant, in turn, that they were looking for a city with a decommissioned or downsized air force base. Airports like this typically still had scheduled commuter service—several flights per day to hubs in Chicago or St. Louis or Minneapolis, which meant that they also had control towers and full safety equipment—but their runways were huge and underused.

And, finally, the Klapmeiers wanted a city that wanted, indeed, needed, them to come, and would make that clear in its financial deal. What Cirrus had to offer was the potential of relatively high-wage manufacturing employment, in areas that had lost just this kind of job over the years. In return the Klapmeiers were looking for a significant financial break—rent, land costs, anything else the city could think of. It was a classic start-up deal.

As they surveyed the upper Midwest, the Klapmeiers came up with half a dozen possibilities and two real finalists. One was Grand Forks, North Dakota, with a large public airport, a nearby, but underused airfield at the Grand Forks air force base, plus a branch of the University of North Dakota that specialized in training pilots and air-traffic controllers. The other was Duluth. Duluth had a branch of the University of Minnesota, several colleges, and a medical complex, plus a huge underused airfield of its own.

Duluth also had a mayor, Gary Doty, who had the very opposite of a laissez-faire philosophy about the city's role in business development. He had put together "Team Duluth," a consortium of business executives, bankers, and civic leaders trying to figure out how to attract new factories and headquarters to Duluth. He had intensified the work of something called the "Duluth 1200 Fund." This was a private nonprofit organization, run by prominent local citizens, that directed the use of public economic-development funds as loans for new ventures. The city persuaded Northwest Airlines to locate a new facility for repairing its Airbus fleet in Duluth, rather than in the other sites it was considering, which included Seattle, Kansas City, and Minneapolis. Norwest Bank expanded its processing center in Duluth. The mayor liked to brag that whenever blizzards closed down bank offices in the rest of Minnesota, people in Duluth would find a way to show up for work. When Lake Superior Paper Industries opened a new mill outside Duluth, it received 24,000 applications for its 400 jobs—the kind of labor market balance start-ups like to hear about. "In the early eighties, this was one of highest unemployment areas in the country," says Tom Cotruvo, the city's manager of business development. "One reason the rate stayed so high was that people did whatever they could to be able to cope and stay. So we never had a decayed urban core the way some places did. And we had a ready labor force."

"In 1993, I heard about a company down in Baraboo that was headed for Grand Forks," says Mayor Doty. He is a big man in his fifties. He looks like an old-style machine politician and has the machine politician's commitment to delivering results. "I contacted them and told them, 'You should be in Duluth.' We had the longest runway in Minnesota. And we had a strong desire to bring them here. At the time, Alan Klapmeier was about to put down money on a house in Grand Forks. But I went to Baraboo, and we worked together with labor leaders, business people, people from the university. And all of them told the Klapmeiers, *This is where you belong.*"

"A lot of people did not take Cirrus seriously," Tom Cotruvo adds. "We took them seriously from the first call. They have that unique drive and ability and ambition you don't often see. I like to make the comparison with the Wright brothers. We took a lot of risk when we invested in Cirrus, but we feel it was a measured risk. And we feel it was a very good risk for our community. We look on it not so much as an investment in the company but an investment in the community."

What was the investment? It was a complicated package deal. In two rounds of financing, the city offset nearly $2 million of the capital costs Cirrus would incur in opening its factory there.[6] The Duluth 1200 Fund invested half a million dollars in Cirrus, as a shareholder, and the city government encouraged local banks to complete financing for the project. There seems to be strong local support for this unapologetic activism in recruiting new business. Certainly the mayor is proud of the way the Cirrus deal turned out. "I really expect that some day they'll be the biggest private employers in Duluth," he told me in 1999. "I believe that some-day I'll sit back in my rocking chair and tell my grandchildren, That company that employs thousands of people? Your grandpa was involved in getting them started."

So Cirrus had a new home. But still it needed money. To raise it, from sources other than friends and family and contacts in Duluth, the Klapmeiers came up with a business plan for what they hoped would be a $10 million round of initial funding in 1994.[7]

The central themes of the business plan were the ones the Klapmeiers stressed throughout the nineties: that Cirrus could make money with high-volume production of relatively low-priced new planes, and that it could sell planes in high volume by giving customers more control over their travel and time. Three decades of stagnation in the small-plane business seemed to have killed the idea of high-volume production sales. Manufacturers built and priced their planes on the Rolls-Royce model, planning to get by on a trickle of annual shipments and, through their prices, guaranteeing that there was no more than a trickle of demand. In their business plan and their public statements the Klapmeiers argued that modernized products, aggressively priced, could bring the market back.

"When I'd make the presentation, people would say, with obvious self-assurance, 'Well, of course, nobody *needs* an air-plane,'" Alan Klapmeier says.

"And my answer is: Well, nobody *needs* anything other than a Dodge Neon for an automobile. But in 1997 there were over 900,000 automobiles sold in North America that exceeded $40,000 in cost. You show me a single person that 'needed' one of those cars. So this idea that people don't need airplanes, and somehow that's a reason for the industry being small, is somewhere between stupid and absurd. In an economy like ours, it's not about need. It's about *choice*. Choice comes down to customer value. Some people value a new Lexus. And other people value a cruise in the Bahamas. Other people value a nice house or a second house. And our airplane, and general aviation, can expand the choices people make."

Klapmeier points out that airplanes are built and maintained in a way that allows them to last longer than even today's durable cars, and that they hold their market value far longer than a car does. It was realistic to say that they could be financed over three times as long a period as a car could—say, fifteen years rather than five. Therefore, Klapmeier concludes, the annual financing costs of one of these $175,000 planes would be about comparable to that of a fancy $65,000 car. If nearly a million people bought cars for more than $40,000—and an even larger number invested even more in second homes—then, Klapmeier says, at least a few hundred thousand could in principle afford his new airplane, if he could show that it had value to them. This is what he hoped his plane, and a general revitalization of the industry, might mean.

On this confident assumption, the business plan laid out a long-term strategy: that Cirrus would become a high-volume, full-line producer of modern aircraft, with models that started with the little SR20 and eventually expanded to include small jet planes.[8] According to initial projections, the SR20s would retail for $130,000, and would have a direct manufacturing cost of $90,000—that is, labor and material costs, excluding finance and overhead. Inevitably, and largely due to almost-inevitable delays in raising money, these crucial aspects of the projection turned out to be overoptimistic. By the time it reached the market in 1999, the base model of the plane was priced at $170,000. About half the price increase came from the inclusion of the parachute and a large moving-map display as standard features. Even at the new price Cirrus was taking a loss on each plane, and would until it got production to at least seven or eight planes per week. But still the company stuck to the premise of the business plan, which was that aggressive, loss-leader pricing would expand the market so quickly that volume economies would kick in. "If I told anyone what I thought the potential was here, they'd think I was crazy," Alan Klapmeier says. "So I just say, Here is a product a lot of people will like."

From early 1994, when the factory opened in Duluth, to 1999, when the first plane went into the first customer's hands, the company's activities proceeded along two related but different paths. The people involved in the company's "real" activities— designing, testing, building, and selling the airplane—moved from strength to strength.

In 1994, the first prototype was put together in the factory in Duluth and shown that summer at the Oshkosh convention.

In 1995, the prototypes made their first flights—and advertisements went out, and orders came in.

In 1996, the company expanded the facilities in Duluth and submitted its formal application for a "type certificate," the beginning of the process in which the FAA tests and approves the planes.

In 1997, the parachute tests were finished—and more than 200 customers had put down deposits on the plane.

In 1998, the company expanded again in Duluth, and built more prototypes—and after extensive testing, got its "type certificate" in October. It had 300 orders in hand.

In 1999 Cirrus endured the disastrous crash that killed Scott Anderson, in early March. But in July it delivered the first plane, and its order list exceeded 350. By the end of the year, the list was over 450.

In 2000 every aspect of the company expanded. The workforce grew to 500. It had delivered more than 100 planes, had an order backlog of more than 700, and was producing planes at a rate of nearly one a day. It also received a "production certificate" from the FAA. This meant approval for Cirrus's system of building, testing, and inspecting the planes, not just approval for the planes themselves, and allowed the company to issue "airworthiness certificates" for each new plane off the line rather than submitting each one to the FAA. This was a significant step toward status as a "real" airplane company. Late in the year it unveiled the second entry in its product line: the SR22, with a bigger engine, higher speed, and longer range than the SR20, and a price tag about $60,000 higher. This was in keeping with the company's original plan to offer a broad line of airplanes. It also would be significantly more profitable for the company for each plane sold. Soon several hundred people had joined the waiting list for the SR22.

Through all of this, Cirrus's buzz and reception within the airplane business was as positive as any entrepreneur might want. In the fall of 2000, the magazine *In Flight USA* ran a cover story on the SR20. It called the plane "A brilliantly executed design just right for today's flying—with excellent safety and performance," and much more in the same vein. At about the same time, the independent publication *Aviation Consumer* gave its "Company of the Year" award to Cirrus and its "Product of the Year" award to the SR20.[9] The tone of coverage was generally adulatory, and with all appropriate allowances for the enthusiasm of any industry's trade press, the reception suggested that this was a breakthrough.[10]

Indeed, the general response was so positive that Cirrus's main PR problem soon became a wave of "Hey, they're not *that* good" counterreaction. The early production models of the plane were turning out to be significantly heavier than promised, which meant their payload was less. The company was chronically over-optimistic in predicting production rates and delivery dates, and customers grumbled about the months and years they spent waiting in line. There were various glitches with suppliers and parts. "If you look at history, products, or politics, evolution has a far better track record of success than revolution," Tom Gibson, senior vice president of Mooney Aircraft, said. "Cirrus is a revolution." Chris Dopp, the president of Mooney, said that Cirrus was "an unproven product with basically zero fleet history. A lot of people have to ask themselves would they put their family in this product, and why they need a 'chute." The rival Lancair company noted on its website that "some companies" felt the need to equip their plane with a parachute. "We chose what we and many others feel is an improved approach to safety.... Our design helps the pilot in not having the need for a parachute."

Nonetheless, by any "real" measure the plane was a startling success. The problems were all on the parallel track: the struggle to raise money to keep building the planes. "With its products and buzz, Cirrus would be a slam-dunk $5 billion IPO if it were a dot-com," Rich Karlgaard, the publisher of *Forbes* and veteran of Silicon Valley start-ups, said in the spring of 2000, when dot-com IPOs were still going strong. Karlgaard also held a place on the waiting list for a Cirrus plane.

Far from a slam-dunk IPO, Cirrus was in a constant search for the next loan or investment to meet the payroll. In February 2001 it ran into the classic bind of the undercapitalized start-up company. For the preceding year it had spent heavily in an attempt to ramp up its production rate. The faster it delivered planes, the sooner it could reach a number of desirable goals. It would bring more revenue into the company. It would near its calculated breakeven point when it was delivering a combination of SR20s and SR22s at a rate of more than one per day. It could position itself to sell future planes faster, since the company's main marketing problem was customers' reluctance to wait two or three years after deciding to buy a shiny new plane.

The all-out attempt to raise the production rate inevitably had uneven effects. Early in 2001, the company found that it was already staffed for one-a-day production when its supply lines and machine tools could not yet support that rate. The company's workforce had grown to 630, from 300 eighteen months earlier. On February 5 the Klapmeiers announced that they would furlough 127 workers, nearly 20 percent of the workforce, while they reorganized the production system and supply lines.

The idea was that most or all of these positions would be refilled within the year, when the other bottlenecks were removed. The reality was that the news came as a huge blow, for a company that was still seen as the local leader of high-tech and that cultivated a Midwest family atmosphere in the plant.

I spoke with Alan Klapmeier by phone soon after this announcement. He was in Miami on yet another fund-raising venture. "The irony is, the financial community has been universally positive about this change," he said. "Of course, in a rational world, they would say: 'That's the right move, now let's get on with the deal.' But there's always some other issue."

The fact that the financial world does not conform to logic as he sees it had become Alan Klapmeier's central theme. "The worst part of raising money is, it is so irrational," Alan Klapmeier told me after the money-raising trip, delivering what was for him the ultimate indictment. "In the end it has so little to do with"—and here his voice took on the tone of a person reading a check list, going down the factors that in his "rational" scheme should have allowed his company to get the money it needed—"whether you have:

a customer
who will pay you
for a product
you can deliver
for a profit."

If a company could tick off all those points in the list, he was saying, the financiers should be able to see the logic of the investment. But no!

"Consider where we are right now," he said late in 2000. "We have 650 SR20s sold, we have refundable deposits on 68 SR22s, so that's a $120 million backlog. The airplane's been certified by the FAA. The airplane is in production. We have our FAA production certificate. Customers are happy with the airplane. This is a product that deserves to be built. And yet today, I couldn't go to a bank and say, A customer is picking up his brand new airplane a week from Monday, will you finance this completely finished plane for a week?

Over the years Klapmeier had raised money mainly one by one from individual investors—many of them in the Duluth area or the upper Midwest, nearly all with some previous connection to aviation. "The vast majority of them are individuals who make their own decisions"—this with a little sneer about the institutional investors who are, in Klapmeier's view, mainly determined to do what everyone else is doing.

"You get a very strong sense that while profit is their first motivation, which isn't bad, it isn't long-term profit that they're looking for. They're looking for next week's profit and forget next year. And, if next week isn't going to be profitable, how can I be someplace where I don't look bad when it isn't? It's like a herd. They want to be just part of the cattle in the middle of the herd. They don't want to be the lead bull. They *like* the idea of breathing the dust of the people in front of them! I've had people admit this, they'd rather get there late when everybody else has been successful than risk being the ones who were trying something new. They let the entrepreneurs become the shock troops that go and get their bodies bloodied in the battle, and then they can come in and walk through the carnage and pick up the flag at the end and say, We won the battle! Here we are! Isn't this great!

"You've got this big long desert in front of you. And you decide it's going to take six gallons of water to get across. But if you only get two gallons, you use half a gallon walking out in the desert, you set one gallon down, and you use the other half a gallon to walk back and try to get more. But you've wasted one gallon. That's basically what we've been doing, just making little forays going out in the desert, and then going back to get more, never having had enough to cross that desert." After a moment he added, "But we will cross it!"

All entrepreneurs have a class grudge against all financiers. There is no question that Cirrus's long struggle for money has been the company's main limitation. With another $10 million in working capital, they could have brought the SR20 to market a year or two earlier. I once thought Klapmeier was going to kill me, and perhaps then kill himself, when I told him about a friend of mine who had received tens of millions in venture capital for an Internet-based company with no obvious "revenue model." With $10 million in hand in the year 2000, Cirrus could have bought more production equipment, delivered more planes, avoided layoffs.

The question now is whether the next stage of struggle between these entrepreneurs and their financiers will give Cirrus the historic role of the Tucker Automobile Corporation, which came up with a better idea about transportation but could not stand up to the big boys of the market, or a role more like Apple Computer's. The niche occupied by Dell Computers—a huge-volume, commodity producer—is not immediately available to Cirrus. As we will see in the next chapter, there's another contender for that role, with advantages that start with large supplies of capital. But the Apple model is an important one: a company that has a loyal following, has a steady presence in the market, and undeniably expands the choices open to its users by its insistence on innovative technology and design. A company in that position is also well-poised to expand when the circumstances are right.

To become the aviation world's Apple would require Cirrus to coexist with its tormentors, the financiers, and from the Klapmeier brothers' perspective the only terms offered have amounted not to coexistence but to capitulation. Venture capitalists keep offering them deals, but in return they naturally want a large equity share in the company. "We're not going to *give this away*," Alan Klapmeier said, in exasperation, when I talked with him on the phone shortly after the layoffs. The deals being offered would, in the brothers' view, make a mockery of the years of living on macaroni and cheese, of all the previous close calls they had survived, of the technical problems for which they had figured out ingenious solutions. Why should moneymen, who think they create wealth by just shuffling assets around, be entitled to a significant share of that? Yet the moneymen were indispensable. Without them, Cirrus would be trekking back and forth across the desert rather than seizing the full opportunity it had created.

From the outside it is easy to say: the Klapmeiers had an obvious choice. They could retain tight control over a relatively small company that was always hamstrung by its lack of money. Or they could accept a smaller share of a much larger, faster-growing, better-capitalized company, which could use its capital to expand production to meet demand, offer new products, develop the next generation of fast, safe, simple airplanes that might sustain an air-taxi industry. The Klapmeiers had progressively transferred shares of their company to investors, so that by the time they introduced the SR22 the family held roughly one third of the total shares. Alan Klapmeier says his family has no illusion of being able to keep the company all to themselves. What drives him crazy about the venture capitalists is that they were the ones asking for total control. "We'll turn the company over to them, and in exchange we'll get to have jobs working here." This is not a deal he or his brother could easily accept. The Klapmeiers faced the classic dilemma of entrepreneurs. Their stiffness, self-reliance, and refusal to listen to conventional opinions had allowed them to survive for more than a decade, employ hundreds of people, and do what dozens of firms had tried and failed to do for thirty years: produce a new, successful small airplane. There is a point when original virtues become liabilities, as Bill Gates learned. The Klapmeiers will soon discover, and with them Cirrus and much of the technology hopes of Duluth, whether they would be wiser to stand firm or adapt.

# Disruptive Technology

Cirrus, for all its financial problems, had by the beginning of 2001 achieved something significant. It had started with a "clean sheet" design for a new plane. Whether because the resulting craft combined so many subtle changes or because, on the contrary, it constituted so large a single leap, it got attention throughout its industry as signaling a change from a stagnant era. While hardly cheap, it offered better value than anything else then on sale, which in turn represented a step toward an idea that lower prices could bring higher volume. Its built-in parachute offered a margin of comfort to the majority of people who were fearful about travel in small planes, and its moving-map displays helped bring to small planes the sort of simplifying technology that had become commonplace in expensive jets.

Perhaps most significant, it existed. For decades people had promised to build new planes, only to wash up on the shoals of certification problems or the realities of financing or manufacturing. By the time it had delivered its one hundredth plane, certified its second model, and booked the order for its 750th plane, all by the end of 2000, Cirrus had established itself as something more than a garage enterprise.

But there were also obvious limits to the Cirrus model, most of them tracing back to the fundamental limit of capital. The Klapmeier brothers had wanted to start with a high-speed, long-range, high-capacity turboprop, their ST50. A plane like this would fly high enough to avoid most weather problems; would go fast enough to be a realistic option for trips of 1,000 miles or more; would be reliable enough, with its turbine engine, to achieve a strong safety record; and would be large enough to be practical for "air taxi" operations—that is, for use with a hired pilot rather than strictly for the tiny minority of enthusiasts who knew how to fly. (When produced in sufficient volume, the SR20 and, even more, the SR22, would also have air-taxi potential. But their lower speeds would make them practical for shorter routes, and their four-seat capacity meant they could take a maximum of three paying customers along with the hired pilot.) The demise of Israviation and Cirrus's chronic difficulty in raising money pushed them away from the ST50 as part of their initial mix and meant that they had to start with the SR20 alone. The new idea was to build a market, build production experience, and build their own cash flow with the SR20, and to keep introducing newer, more powerful models until they offered the full product line they originally envisioned.

So a race was on. Cirrus knew where it wanted to get, and it wondered if the established manufacturers would notice the demand for modernized, simplified, more reasonably priced airplanes before Cirrus could get there first. We're not trying to take anyone's sales away, Alan Klapmeier would say time and again. We think there's an untapped new market with more sales for everybody. Still, if the company's basic idea was right, and there really was a pent-up demand for a safe, comfortable, reasonably priced alternative to airline travel, then sooner or later other entrepreneurs would direct their efforts accordingly.

In the springtime of 2000, the industry was startled by the appearance of just such an entrepreneurial firm, and one with advantages in precisely the areas where Cirrus was struggling. The new company was named Eclipse Aviation, and it had an unusual corporate structure. The dozen members of its sales, finance, and senior management teams operated from a modern building just off the main runway at Albuquerque's international airport. More than one hundred engineers and designers creating what would be Eclipse's plane were based 1,500 miles away, in a suburb of Detroit named Walled Lake.[1]

What Cirrus believed its SR20 had shown at the "entry-level" end of the market, Eclipse hoped that its Eclipse 500 would show at a more costly and sophisticated level. The SR20 applied a generation's worth of advances in electronics and aerodynamics to create a new light airplane. The Eclipse 500 was designed to apply mechanical innovations that came from the defense-contracting industry, plus engineering and manufacturing concepts from the automobile industry, and design techniques and venture capital from the modern software industry, to produce "disruptive technology" of a fundamental sort.

What Eclipse claimed to offer was the first small jet plane cheap enough to make a difference in a national transportation system. With its new approach to computerized aircraft design, its new "lean manufacturing" systems, and its dramatically new jet engine, it promised to market a plane for well under one-third the cost of preceding models. Because this plane would be a jet, it could be fast enough and safe enough to attract ordinary civilian travelers. Because it would be cheap, it could provide the hardware for a nationwide network of "air taxis" or "air limos," which could pick up passengers at local airports and take them direct to their destinations. Because it would be small, it could land at nearly any of 6,000 to 8,000 airports in North America, rather than the 600-odd that now have scheduled commercial service of any sort. And because it was designed to hold five people (comfortably) or six (in a pinch), it could position itself as the SUV of the air, with a hired pilot up front and a small family or business group in the rear.

It could do all these things … if its plans worked. In the springtime of 2001, Eclipse was still in the exhilarating "promise" stage of the product cycle. It could excite customers and investors with projections of what its airplane would do, rather than, like Cirrus, having to repair the inevitable bugs and apologize for the inevitable delays. Its envious rivals said that Eclipse was bringing to the airplane business the computer industry's trick of "vaporware." Vaporware is a wonderful-sounding program whose only drawback is that it doesn't actually exist. Time and again software companies have promised fabulous new releases of their products "real soon now," hoping that this will distract interest, money, and investment away from potential competitors. The Safire Aircraft company, which hoped to produce a plane like the Eclipse, felt itself particularly harmed by Eclipse's rosy promises.

Nonetheless, enough has gone Eclipse's way to earn it the benefit of the doubt. Compared with Cirrus, the company is better financed, and its executives are vastly better-connected in the established business world. To apply the computer analogy once again, if Cirrus could be thought of as an airborne Apple, giving early hints of what "personal" air travel might mean, Eclipse was positioning itself as Dell or Compaq, hoping to use money and marketing to do business on a huge scale. With Cirrus, the Klapmeier brothers have recapitulated the classic American start-up story—including the significant advantage of having family funds to draw on first. Eclipse's is a tale of industrial strength in one field being adapted and applied to another. One of the two men most responsible for its creation is in his early fifties and had spent most of his previous career as a software entrepreneur. The other turned eighty in 2001 and had been a leading defense contractor through the cold war. These men, Vern Raburn and Sam Williams, believed that they and the team they assembled could change the way many millions of people travel.

Vern Raburn has been interested in aviation nearly all of his life, but until the late nineties had made his living in various aspects of computing. Raburn was born in Oklahoma in 1950, and grew up in Southern California. His father worked for Douglas Aircraft, later to become part of McDonnell-Douglas, which in turn became part of Boeing. After the launch of *Sputnik* in 1957, when Raburn was in elementary school, his father went to work on space projects. "He spent his whole career developing a new industry, space, just like I did in the PC business," Raburn says. Raburn studied aeronautical engineering and industrial technology at Cal Poly San Luis Obispo and Cal State Long Beach, and then spent his twenties through his midforties making it in the computer and software business. He is a medium-height, stocky man with glasses. His manner is to deliver a constant stream of wisecracks.

In 1976 Raburn opened the Byte Shop, only the third computer store in the greater Los Angeles area. Shortly thereafter he joined the newly formed Microsoft Corporation and became head of its consumer products division. Dottie Hall, whom he had met several years earlier and eventually married in 1986, worked for Microsoft at the same time and developed its marketing and public relations department. Although Raburn and Hall left the company before its era of greatest growth, from the mideighties through the midnineties, they never seriously had to worry about money after that. "We don't talk about our financial position," Raburn said in an e-mail message when I asked about the scale of his holdings. "Suffice it to say that between Microsoft, Lotus, and Symantec [his two next companies] we accumulated enough wealth to live comfortably. I am not the zillionaire that the world believes I am. But I've done OK."

Over the next fifteen years, Raburn was a "serial executive," spending several years as a senior official at one software company and then moving to another. He was an executive vice president at Lotus Development, involved in the launch of its successful spreadsheet program, 1-2-3. Then he was chairman and CEO of the Symantec Corporation, another influential software company. In 1990 he raised money from venture capitalists to start the Slate Corporation. This was an early attempt to develop and market a handheld computer that could accept handwritten instructions—that is, something like what is now known as the Palm Pilot. The Slate project failed, as all handheld projects failed until the introduction of the Palm Pilot in the late nineties. In 1994 Raburn sold Slate's remaining assets to Compaq.

Next Raburn went to work for Paul Allen, the cofounder of Microsoft, as president of the Paul Allen Group. Allen held the second largest number of Microsoft shares, after Bill Gates, and as Microsoft's share price soared through the nineties his assets were worth as much as $30 billion. During the time Raburn was working for him, Allen became the third-richest person in America, after Bill Gates and the investor Warren Buffett, and one of the ten richest people in the world. Raburn's responsibility at the PAG was to find and manage investment opportunities in emerging-technology companies. (Another of Allen's holding firms, Vulcan Ventures, managed investments in sports, entertainment, and media companies.) As the market for electric utilities was deregulated in the nineties, Raburn became an executive of Capstone Turbine Corporation, which designed small, light, efficient turbines that would let companies generate their own power efficiently from natural gas.

The constants in Raburn's transient-seeming professional life had been his taste for starting new ventures and his interest in technology. Another constant was his interest in flying. "I am," he said when I first met him, "an aviation nut." He learned to fly as a teenager, soloing when he was seventeen and earning his license shortly after he reached the minimum age of eighteen. When he started making money he indulged his taste for airplanes. In 1987 he and his wife bought a Lockheed Constellation from the actor John Travolta. The Constellation is the most surreally beautiful of the prejet airliners, with its distinctive triple tail and salmon-shaped fuselage.

The Travolta plane had been a military rather than civilian-airline model, and had taken part in the Berlin airlift. Raburn and Hall paid Travolta roughly $100,000 for the plane but spent at least $1 million over the next decade refurbishing it. By 1990 they had launched a quixotic business of flying it around the country

Vern Raburn's Lockheed Constellation, bought from John Travolta.

and charging onlookers for tours or rides. As part of the commemoration of the fiftieth anniversary of the Airlift, in 1998, Raburn flew the Constellation into Berlin's Tempelhof Airport. By the time he turned fifty, in 2000, Raburn had accumulated more than 5,000 flying hours and was qualified in fifteen kinds of aircraft, including the World War II–vintage B-25 and A-26, plus most two- and four-engine piston airliners.

In the midnineties, when Raburn was working for Paul Allen, he was traveling around the country for board meetings and to look at companies Allen was interested in. Many of these were in "nonhub" locations—Lancaster, Pennsylvania, or Ithaca, New York. At first Raburn made these trips by commercial airline, in addition to commuting every week to Seattle from his home in Arizona, but after about a year he told Allen that he couldn't stand the hub-and-spoke agonies anymore. Allen had bought a Citation Jet—Cessna's very popular entry in the corporate-jet market, whose basic model costs $3.8 million—and made it available to Raburn. Raburn was checked out as a pilot of the Citation, he equipped the interior as a mobile office, and he spent another year flying it from place to place for his visits. The quickest commercial connection from Ithaca to Lancaster, a US Airways commuter flight, via the hub in Pittsburgh, takes five hours. From takeoff to touchdown in the Citation was barely thirty minutes. Allen himself had his own Boeing 757 to use for point-to-point travel.

Among his many interests, Allen had long been fascinated with space travel. In 1996, Raburn heard that Burt Rutan was also shifting his attention that way. Rutan, who like Raburn had been an undergraduate at Cal Poly San Luis Obispo in the sixties, had through the seventies and eighties been the most celebrated creator of innovative airplane designs. In the nineties, contemptuous of NASA's slow pace in space flight, he began thinking about craft that could fly beyond the air. With possible joint ventures between Allen and Rutan in mind, Raburn flew to Rutan's headquarters in the Mojave Desert.

"Of course, they were looking on me as Mr. Moneybags," Raburn says of the meeting; that was his natural identity when he represented Allen. "They thought that I might be the one who could save them from the eternal struggle for capital in the aircraft business." During the visit, while talking about the commercial and scientific aspects of space travel, Rutan asked Raburn whether he had met Sam Williams. Of course he'd heard of him, Raburn said. Well, you really ought to get together, Rutan told him—a suggestion that was the beginning of the Eclipse corporation.

Vern Raburn had heard of Sam Williams because Raburn's office was stacked with copies of *Aviation Week* and *Jane's* military journals, and to be interested in military aircraft was to be in awe of what Williams had done.

Williams was born in 1921 in Seattle, raised in Columbus, Ohio, and trained in mechanical engineering at Purdue before World War II. Since then he has devoted his working life to studying, developing, and perfecting turbine engines. In the forties he worked at Chrysler, developing gas-turbine engines for airplanes and for an experimental turbine-powered car. "The automotive turbine engine got a lot of publicity in the automotive media in those days," Williams says. "I saw the opportunity of developing small engines for aircraft, but Chrysler wasn't interested. So I decided to start my own organization."

In 1954 he established his company, Williams Research, outside Detroit, with three employees. The company grew as it built turbine engines for a variety of uses—boats, helicopters, airplanes, and even a military jeep. Williams's dream of developing a practical turbine-powered car for Detroit's big auto manufacturers was never realized. But his company, eventually known as Williams International, became a more and more important vendor of turbine engines to the military, in particular an engine that was largely responsible for introducing a whole new class of weaponry. That engine was originally used to power an oddball personal-transport device, but its real significance was in making possible the cruise missile.

During World War II, the German military had developed the V-1 "buzz bomb," which flew the 150-plus miles from launch sites in northern Europe across the English Channel toward London. The weapons were crude but cheap enough that the Nazis could build and launch 10,000 of them in the final year of the war. Nearly a quarter hit London or its environs.

During the cold war years, the U.S. military was determined to exploit the potential of nonpiloted flying weapons that were far more sophisticated than the V-1. These "cruise missiles" would be able to fly long distances, at altitudes low enough to escape radar detection, and with guidance accurate enough to take them close to important targets. So-called strategic cruise missiles would carry nuclear warheads, as a complement to the other elements of the U.S. strategic force: land-based nuclear missiles, nuclear bombs carried by bomber airplanes, and sea-launched nuclear missiles carried on submarines. The engines for strategic cruise missiles, along with their guidance systems, would obviously have to be super-reliable, so that the nuclear warheads were sure to reach their targets and not go anywhere else. "Tactical" cruise missiles would carry conventional explosive warheads.

The U.S. military began serious development of cruise missiles during the Carter administration, and they entered the arsenal in the early Reagan years. Two forms of technological progress had made them possible. One was the dramatic change in electronics and computing power, which gave the missiles far more effective ways of finding their targets.[2] The other was the creation of an engine small enough, light enough, and efficient enough in its use of fuel to let the missiles travel to targets 1,500 miles or more away. This engine was Sam Williams's F-107 "turbofan."

A turbofan is, essentially, a variation on the traditional turbojet engine that gets more thrust for a given amount of fuel.[3] Turbofans are more complicated and delicate to build than turbojets, and early in the planning process for the cruise missile, the big, established engine-building companies like General Electric told the military that it was impossible to build a turbofan small enough to fit the cruise missile. This jeopardized the entire cruise missile plan, because a normal turbojet would use too much fuel to give the weapon a reasonable range.

Sam Williams's turbine engines, as first applied to personal transportation.

The solution came from Sam Williams. In the late sixties he had patented a very small turbofan engine, which the U.S. military considered for use as a "personal jetpack" transportation device.

The personal jetpack, an early variant of which was featured in the James Bond film *Thunderball*, never made it into military service.[4] But, as the statement inducting Williams into the National Aviation Hall of Fame in 1998 said, "This engine was the forerunner to today's cruise missile engines. Sam's privately funded work convinced the Air Force and Navy that these engines were feasible to propel missiles to great distances at low altitude. His inventive genius made cruise missiles possible, and to date cruise missile engine production has exceeded 6,000." The cruise missiles in the U.S. arsenal are powered by the small F-107 turbofan engine from Williams International. In the lobby of Williams International's factory in Walled Lake, virtually the only part of a highly secure defense-contract site most visitors are allowed to see, two personal notes from U.S. presidents to Sam Williams hang on the walls. One is from Jimmy Carter, and the other from Ronald Reagan, both thanking Williams for inventing the engine that made cruise missiles possible. In the same display room are the plaques and medals indicating Sam Williams's unprecedented sweep of the four main honors in his field: the Collier Trophy, which he received in 1978; the Wright Brothers Memorial Trophy, 1988; the President's National Medal of Technology, 1995, for "his unequaled achievements as a gifted inventor, tenacious entrepreneur, risk-taker and engineering genius"; and his induction into the Aviation Hall of Fame.

When I asked Williams himself how important his engine had been in the cruise missile program, he responded in an awkwardly precise way that recalled the style of his fellow engineer Jimmy Carter: "The requirement was for an engine that could fly a great distance at low altitudes. We had developed such an engine that was way ahead of what anyone else could do. We won four different competitions for the cruise missile program, and that enabled us to produce the engines for both the navy and the air force. They gave us credit for making the program feasible."

In the eighties and early nineties, Williams began thinking about how to apply his engine technology to civilian transport. The great challenge in general aviation, as he saw it, was similar to the one the military faced with the cruise missile: how to make modern, efficient propulsion systems available on a small scale. "I saw an opportunity for making turbofan engines that would be lighter and smaller, and lower in cost, than any then available for commercial uses," he told me. "I believed that if we could produce such an engine we could generate a new category of small commercial jets in the same way that our engines had generated a new category of unmanned military craft."

On this principle, through the early and mideighties Williams International spent several hundred million dollars of its own research funds to develop a new, small engine called the FJ44. (The company is privately held, mainly by the Williams family, so the investment was essentially the family's own money.) The FJ44 was an enormous commercial success and became the dominant business-jet engine of the nineties. Cessna, Raytheon, and other manufacturers designed new planes to take advantage of it. These planes, the most popular of which was the Cessna CitationJet, cost several million dollars apiece.

But Williams wanted to take a more dramatic step, and in the late eighties, again with the company's own funds, he began work on an engine he called the FJX. What would be extraordinary about this would be its size. The popular FJ44s, used in Cessna Citations and other heavy, expensive planes, produced from 1,900 to 2,400 pounds of thrust per engine, depending on the model, and weighed 400 pounds and up themselves. That is, their thrust-to-weight ratio was 4 or 5 to 1. Williams's goal was an engine that produced about one-third as much thrust, 700 pounds per engine, but that weighed around 80 pounds, for a previously unheard of thrust-to-weight ratio of 9 to 1.

If he could achieve this compact propulsion system, he thought, changes in nearly everything else about aviation would follow. "We at Williams International believed that there was potentially a very large market for high performance, lower cost, lightweight, entry-level jet-powered general aviation aircraft to replace propeller- and piston-powered aircraft," he said in 2000, in one of his rare public statements, an appearance before a congressional committee studying the future of aviation. "New low-cost, high-performance, fuel-efficient turbofan engines would have to be developed if we were to revitalize the country's business jet and general aviation industry."[5] In 2001 he told me: "With the success of the FJ44, we concluded that we could make feasible even smaller light jets, down in the light aircraft category, planes with 4,000 to 5,000 pound gross weight." These days, the only planes that light have piston engines. Williams believed that with a supersmall jet engine light jets could become practical.

Williams generally avoids interviews, and I hurriedly arranged a trip to Walled Lake when he finally agreed to talk with me. At the last minute a travel obligation arose for just that time, so while I saw the factory I spoke with him only on the phone. In photos he is a serious-looking man resembling the elder George Bush, with grey hair combed back from a high forehead. On the telephone he spoke in a virtual whisper, so that I had to keep the receiver pressed to my ear in order to hear him. "A man used to being listened to," one of his associates said the next day when I asked if he had been sick.

Williams believed that his company should always and only make turbine engines, not cruise missiles or boats or airplanes or anything else. But sometimes the airplane companies were slower to recognize the potential of his engines than he would have liked. So as a way of stimulating interest in a new kind of small jet that might use his new small engines, starting in the early nineties he used Williams International's internal assets to design, build, and test a prototype small jet. He had taken a similar approach a few years earlier, when developing the market for the FJ44 engine, and he thought it would pay off with the new, smaller engine as well. "We built the prototype," he told me, "with no intention of really producing airplanes ourselves but with the objective of stimulating the interest of major airplane manufacturers in developing their own small business jets around the capability of our small turbofan engine."[6]

By 1994, Williams's company was working on an engine that would weigh well under 100 pounds, would provide 700 pounds of thrust, and when used in pairs would propel a small jet. For ideas about the design of the plane that would show off this engine's potential, Williams turned, as he had before, to the acknowledged visionary-design leader of the light aircraft business, Burt Rutan. In the eighties Rutan had designed a working prototype plane that demonstrated what the previous Williams engine, the FJ44, could do. Williams was confident that Rutan could do it again.

By the springtime of 1997, Rutan's Scaled Composites company had created a flying model of this new plane, which was called the V-Jet II. It was based on Williams's own concepts and had a self-consciously futuristic look. The wings were swept forward, toward the nose of the plane, rather than back. The tail was in the shape of a large V, something rarely seen in small planes since Beech had tried the design on its Bonanza in the fifties. It was somewhat cramped inside—in theory it held five passengers, but only if one of the five was more or less sitting in another passenger's lap—and it was powered by existing Williams engines, since the full, working model of the very light engine was still being developed. This meant that it could not go as high or fast as Williams thought a revolutionary new, small jet should be able to. But it did fly, and to Williams it did indicate the future.

It was with the V-Jet in mind that Burt Rutan had asked Vern Raburn: Say, do you know Sam Williams? Williams's company had a lot of money, but not enough to finance a whole aircraft project on its own. Perhaps Mr. Moneybags, in the form of

Raburn's influence over Allen's assets, could make the difference for them. Early in 1997, Raburn and Allen traveled together to Mojave to talk with Rutan—about space travel, Allen thought. While they were there he showed them the mockup of the V-Jet.

"It was off in the corner behind plywood walls," Raburn told me. "We finally got a look at it, and I remember thinking, This is *soooooo cool!*"

"Paul looked at it, and sort of went, *Ehhhh?* We'd flown to Mojave from Seattle in his 757—just the two of us, plus two pilots and the flight attendants. So I am looking at it and thinking, 'Wow!,' and he is thinking of the 757 and saying, 'Nice little airplane.'"

Their different reactions to the V-Jet were an omen. A few months later, Raburn and Allen agreed to an amicable separation. When Raburn told Rutan and Williams about this, they were initially crestfallen—no more Mr. Moneybags!—but the three of them continued their discussions about the possibilities for a new kind of aviation. At that year's Oshkosh show, in late July 1997, Raburn took his trusty old Constellation for display—and found

The V–Jet II, inspiration for the Eclipse.

that its assigned space on the tarmac was immediately next to that of the V-Jet II, which was making its debut. Maybe this was an omen too.

At this point Bruce Holmes, Dan Goldin, and NASA reentered the picture. The three big programs that Holmes had kicked off, with Goldin's support, at NASA were the Advanced General Aviation Transportation Experiments, or AGATE, which included the innovations in wing design, flight instruments, crashworthiness, and safety that were applied by Cirrus, Lancair, and others; the Small Aircraft Transportation System, or SATS, which was meant to go into action in the early 2000s and would prepare the nationwide network of small airports to handle larger volumes of small planes; and the General Aviation Propulsion project, or GAP. Part of the GAP program was to become a de facto partnership between NASA and Williams International.

The historic idea behind GAP is that the major advances in air transportation have mainly come from advances in propulsion. Propellers to jets, early turbojets to modern, efficient turbofans, steady improvements in reliability. The unpleasant reality of small-plane aviation is that most planes costing less than, say, $2 million in the late nineties were on the unmodernized side of this divide. The imbalance is like that in the computing world in the sixties, when semiconductor technology was replacing transistors and even vacuum tubes. Customers who could afford big, industrial-scale computers from IBM or Univac could take advantage of the huge increase in reliability that semiconductors brought. Small business or home enthusiasts coped with vacuum tubes that blew out and soldered connections that broke. Personal-scale computing took off only in the late seventies, when the power and reliability of semiconductors became available on a wide scale. Something roughly comparable is what GAP hoped to bring to the aviation world.

The piston engines that still drive most sub-million-dollar planes—the aviation equivalents of vacuum tubes—have several fundamental limitations. They are noisy. They are heavy, relative to the thrust they provide. Although they have gotten steadily more reliable decade by decade, they still are dramatically less dependable than turbine engines, mainly because they have so many more moving parts. Every pilot in primary training goes through countless "engine out" drills, in which the instructor pulls the throttle to idle, says "Oh! You've just lost your engine!" and coaches the student pilot in how to find a suitable flat landing place and glide the plane in.[7] Nearly every pilot is first licensed to fly in a single-engine plane. Most of the training involved in being licensed for multiengine planes involves learning what to do if one of the engines fails and the plane is suddenly exposed to much more thrust from one side of the plane than the other. In real life, sudden engine failures for reasons other than fuel exhaustion are rare. But the idea that the engine could fail at any time plays a major role in small-plane training, and the awareness of this risk plays a major part in small-plane use.

By contrast, turbine engines, with their small number of moving parts, have become so reliable that a leading reason for in-flight failure is that some foreign object—often a bird—has been sucked through the system, breaking off turbine blades. This is why "bird strike tests," in which carcasses of turkeys or chickens are fired into test engines running at full speed, are an important part of certifying new engines. The engine has to show that it can handle this disruption without destroying the plane.

The traditional piston engines have an additional problem: they run on a kind of fuel that is harder and harder to find. When a turbine engine, either a jet or a turboprop, is operating nearby, the whole area smells like kerosene, since turbine planes run on a distillate, usually one called Jet Fuel A, that is a variety of kerosene. Piston planes run on a kind of gasoline called "100 Low Lead." It is similar to automotive gas, but with a higher octane count, 100 versus the high-80s typical of modern cars, and, despite the name, also a higher lead content than today's automotive gasoline. In the late nineties, additive companies simply stopped producing some of the ingredients necessary to distill 100LL. When the existing stock of additive runs out, sometime between 2005 and 2010, that will be it for the fuel on which most current piston engines run. (Many of the engines can be adapted to use a different mix of fuel. Some, especially turbocharged models, cannot.)

So part of the ambition of NASA's GAP program was "reform" rather than "revolution"—that is, creating a kind of piston engine that would be more reliable than the current versions and could run on cheaper, more readily available jet fuel. This it planned to do with a new class of quiet, efficient engines that would run on diesel fuel.[8]

The "revolution" part of the GAP scheme was the attempt to leap past piston technology altogether and make turbine engines practical for sub-million-dollar small planes. The "primary goal" of this part of the program, NASA said, was "reducing the price of small turbine engines by a factor of 10 (from hundreds of thousands to tens of thousands of dollars)."[9]

Toward that end, NASA through the GAP program made an agreement with Williams International in 1996. "The administrator of NASA [Dan Goldin] believed that the light aircraft market could be revived if there were available a light, small turbofan engine that was not available at that time," Sam Williams said of this arrangement. "So he put up a competition to share the cost of development between NASA and the company. We won that competition, and we were on our way." Williams International brought to the deal the FJX engine it had been developing, with all the sunk development costs. NASA would put up $38 million for further progress on the engine, with the proviso that Williams spend at least that much more itself.[10]

The engine that came from this work, known by Williams as the EJ22, would not by itself accomplish NASA's long-term goal for jet propulsion: a 90 percent cost reduction in cost per unit of thrust. Still, by the time a preview version was announced at the Oshkosh show in the summer of 1997, it was recognized as a genuine breakthrough, because of its unprecedented "thrust-to-weight" performance. The big turbofan engines used in Boeing and Airbus planes develop tens of thousands of pounds of thrust—but they weigh many thousands of pounds themselves. The most powerful of them have a thrust-to-weight ratio between 6 and 7; most are between 4 and 5. A top-of-the-line Gulfstream V-Jet, for instance, has two engines made by BMW-Rolls-Royce that each produce 16,500 pounds of thrust. But each engine weighs 3,500 pounds, for a thrust-to-weight ratio of 4.7 to 1. This would make the new Williams engine, with its promised 9-to-1 ratio, an unprecedented achievement.

Exactly how Williams accomplished this breakthrough is something about which his company says virtually nothing and Vern Raburn, his initial customer, says very little. "You will notice that in all the aviation magazines you've never seen a cutaway drawing of the FJ44," Vern Raburn says, referring to Williams's previous engine, which had been used on thousands of planes. "Sam is not reclusive as an individual, but corporately there is tremendous reclusiveness—just a way of business they've learned from defense contracting, and also the way they maintain their competitive advantage."

Early in 2001, I was given a chance to walk through the Williams International factory in Walled Lake, a degree of openness the company usually resists. But if I wanted even this glimpse, I had to agree to consider the visit the equivalent of a "deep background" or even "off the record" conversation. I was allowed to get a sense of how the place looked and what sort of machines it contained, but not to describe in any detail the work that was going on there. This was frustrating but, I thought, preferable to not seeing it at all. What I can say is that everything I saw was consistent with the company's official explanation of how it had been able to squeeze so much power out of engines so small and light.

The official explanation is that the engines succeed not because of any single dramatic step, comparable to splitting the atom or harnessing steam power, but instead because of the accumulated effect of many years' worth of refinement in design, manufacturing, and quality control. "There's no one element that makes these light engines feasible," Sam Williams says. "Just continuous, steady improvement in fans, compressors, combustion chambers, turbines, control systems, all of the elements that make up an engine." For example, a crucial element in any turbine engine is the compressor. This is a series of fans, closely spaced together, which compress the air more and more tightly, in several stages, before the fuel is introduced for combustion. In a traditional turbine engine, a compressor might include several thousand parts, hundreds of which would be the individual turbine blades. Williams found a way to machine its entire compressor for the new engine out of a single piece of titanium, whose final weight was less than one and one-quarter pounds. Other companies now do the same thing. The difference is that Williams has learned to do it faster, more carefully, with a lower defect rate, than anyone else.

"The magic of what Williams has done on this engine—and it has taken them forty years of development to do it—is absolutely analogous to the semiconductor business," says Vern Raburn, who frequently describes his current business of airplanes by reference to his past business of computers. "You take Intel," the world's dominant maker of microprocessing chips. "The real magic of Intel is the fab process"—the "fabrication" system through which

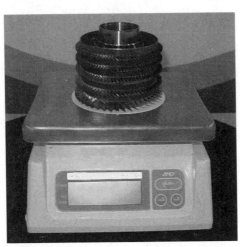

The Williams Engine Compressor, made from a single piece of metal and weighing less than one and one quarter pounds.

they actually build the chips. "They bring the line width on the chips from three microns, to two microns, to point-seven, to point-three-five, and they're always the first ones out there with the newest process, that produces the highest yield at these new levels." The analogy in continual refinement of engines involves, among other things, "tip clearances"—the distance between the end of the spinning turbine blades and the casing in which they are housed. The closer the tips can come to the casing, without touching, the more efficient the engine will be. Williams has brought the tolerances down to levels other companies have not.

"What Intel has done is what Williams has done. They've figured out how to build an engine that's just been shrunk down. They have developed new machinery that allows them not only to maintain the tolerances as the sizes shrink, but also radically to improve the throughput on the machine, which ultimately translates directly into cost."

As I walked through the factory, observing (as I believe I can safely say) machinists and technicians walk around in work jackets with "Williams International" embroidered in script across the back, and seeing a giant-size American flag suspended over one door, I felt I had been transported to some pre-1968, pre–riot-and-disruption version of America. Perhaps this is the way Project Apollo factories looked in the early sixties. Teamwork in an observable, mechanical sense, carried out by people who were continually solving new technical challenges. When I have visited semiconductor factories or dot-com start-ups, I have often felt a strange sense of letdown. They look just the way you think they would, from reading about them so often. A modern manufacturing plant, full of computerized machine tools and laser-guided metal-cutting systems, is more startling because it is so rarely represented in media or culture.

So these were the forces in place as of late 1997. NASA wanted a better jet engine, and had contracted with Williams to produce it. Sam Williams had an idea of how this engine could become the basis of a new kind of low-cost jet, which could revolutionize business travel, the mock-up of which he'd developed with Burt Rutan. Vern Raburn was preparing for another of his career shifts and was fascinated by the idea of the project that Williams and Rutan had underway. Each of the principals describes it as a moment when all the forces had come together in the right way.

"Once we had won some of the earlier battles," for design experiments like those carried out by Cirrus and Lancair, "we realized we had to make progress with engines," Bruce Holmes says. "And Sam Williams had a vision for what his small engines would do, which he got Dan Goldin excited about."

Sam Williams says, "Vern Raburn and I hit it off immediately, because he had the same vision that we had, and that Dan Goldin had." That vision, Williams says, is that "he could generate a huge new business market for turbofan-powered light airplanes in the 4,000- to 5,000-pound gross weight category"—that is, less than half as heavy, and less than one-third as expensive, as anything on the market.

And Vern Raburn says, "The more I talked to Sam about the engine, the more interested I became. We knew that propulsion is the fountainhead from which everything else flows. And here is the guy who has proven to the world that you can build itty-bitty turbofans—and who has always delivered them on time and under budget. If there is somebody who can pull this off, this is the guy."

By the end of 1997, nearly six months after the Oshkosh adventure, and three years before the Oshkosh 2000 meeting at which they would actually unveil the plane, Raburn agreed to go to work with Williams. The corporate structure would be fairly odd. Raburn would be the CEO and president of the company that would eventually produce and sell the new airplanes. Initially the company was called Pronto Personal Jets. The name Eclipse occurred, in a casual brainstorming session, early in 2000, just before the company had to go to press with the marketing and PR materials announcing their intentions to build the new jet. ("You're talking about eclipsing the competition," a friend had said to Peter Reed, one of the company's executives, when they were talking about its plans in the stands at a high school wrestling tournament. "Why not call it Eclipse?")

But, at least as Sam Williams envisioned the relationship, Pronto/Eclipse would for the foreseeable future consist only of Raburn himself. Williams International, with its team of experienced engineers, would continue testing and refining the new jet engine, and preparing it for final FAA certification. Williams would also hire a team of aeronautical engineers to test and refine the Eclipse airplane itself, and prepare it for FAA certification. Meanwhile, Raburn would raise money, publicize the plane, and take advance orders. Only when the plane was tested, approved, and ready would production work shift to the Eclipse company. From that point on, Williams would build and sell as many engines as Eclipse could use, and Eclipse would be a stand-alone airplane company, with its manufacturing, sales, and management headquarters in Albuquerque.

The deal came with semiodd financial arrangements too, although nothing is truly unusual in the chronically cash-starved world of aircraft construction. Williams had already sunk tens of millions of dollars in preliminary design and testing for its new engine, and the contract under the GAP program, from NASA, had brought in tens of millions more. But taking the engine to full commercial readiness would require extra tens of millions, and the full development costs of the jet would be in the hundreds of millions before it was ready to go on sale. These costs the new Eclipse company would pay—assuming that Raburn could raise the money. In return it would get a revolutionary new product to sell, and would have a strategic advantage over competitors. The most important single ingredient in the new, light, cheap jet was the new, light, cheap Williams engine—and for a limited number of years, Williams would provide the engine to Eclipse alone. Established players like Cessna or Raytheon, innovators like Cirrus or Lancair or Safire, outsiders like Honda or Toyota, couldn't jump right in to challenge Eclipse, because they wouldn't have the Williams mini-engine.

As relations between Williams and Raburn evolved, the corporate structure shifted slightly. Month by month operating responsibilities were transferred slowly to Eclipse, rather than waiting for an all-at-once transfer when the plane was ready for sale. This was in keeping with Raburn's idea that they were not just creating a new airplane; they were also trying to create a successful start-up company, which would have some coherence when it moved into its ultimate operating headquarters in Albuquerque. But the fundamental financial arrangements remained as originally planned, and that meant that Raburn had to get busy finding investors.

In the midnineties, Raburn had been talking with Mike Maples, a two-decade veteran of IBM who had been brought in as a senior official at Microsoft. They had been discussing a new book called *Startup*, by Jerrold Kaplan, which described how annoying it was to compete against Microsoft. Maples was complaining about the book, and gave this illustration of what was wrong with it: "If you believed that book, he spent three-quarters of his time raising money." Maples, of course, had not spent his career at start-ups. Raburn, who had, replied, "Mike, that's the part of the book that sounds really accurate to me."

Like Alan Klapmeier, Raburn faced the fundamental challenge of persuading investors to give him a chance to create his new machine. His job was harder than Klapmeier's, because he needed to raise so much more money. Raburn expected he would need to raise more than $300 million before the plane went on sale, versus about one-quarter that much for Cirrus. But it was also much easier, because of the connections that he and Sam Williams brought to the deal.

Williams's ties were to the world of traditional manufacturing. Although he had been frustrated in his dream of enticing auto companies to put his turbine engines in their cars, he had extensive connections throughout Detroit. He was able to bring Harold "Red" Poling, a former CEO of Ford, onto Eclipse's board of directors and to attract investment from others in the industry. More generally, the reputation Williams International had established in forty years of providing engines to both military and commercial customers—supplying them on time, on budget, and with technical advances over competitors—made investors more likely to give the proposal a serious hearing.

Raburn's most important connections were to the world of software money. Both Bill Gates and Paul Allen invested in Eclipse, along with less famous technology figures. He also knew other computer people who thought the time had finally come to apply the last quarter century's worth of electronic advances to aviation. One such partner was Dan Schwinn, who in 1985, at the age of twenty-three, had founded the Shiva company. Shiva became an early leader in computer networking; when it went public a decade later, Schwinn was suddenly rich. Schwinn became a pilot, and he decided to start a company, called Avidyne, that aspired to apply advanced graphics and electronics to aviation systems. Raburn contacted him, and they agreed they might work on integrating Avidyne's systems into Raburn's new planes.

As he made his pitches for money, Raburn played both defense and offense. He had a positive presentation to make about the company's prospects, but first he had to defend himself against the financial world's belief that money invested in new airplanes was money thrown away.

On the defensive side, Raburn anticipated objections by ticking off the reasons why most aircraft companies had failed, and explaining why things would be different for Eclipse. Companies that had gone into this business had typically made several operations mistakes, he said.

One was to underestimate how much money it would take to enter the market. The result of this wishful thinking was to spend years cutting corners and operating with too little money. The Klapmeiers could tell him all about this, even though they were among the most successful of all aircraft start-ups. "Usually these companies have failed because they *grossly* underestimate the capital needed to certify and build an airplane," says Peter Reed, an experienced corporate financier who joined Eclipse in 2000 to handle fund-raising. "They try to do it on a shoestring because they just love aviation so much. They're aviation nuts first and businessmen second. What's different about Eclipse is that we love aviation—you can't be more of a plane nut than Vern—but first and foremost we're business people." Cirrus had delivered fifty planes by the time it had used $70 million in capital. Eclipse set a target of $60 million for its initial, "angel" round of financing from interested individuals. It then planned for a second round of $120 million (which it achieved late in 2000) and total estimated investment of $300 million before the plane first came to market.

The second chronic problem that brought down aviation start-ups, Raburn said, was "poor execution." This category included all the glitches in planning, purchasing, delivery, maintenance, and quality control that kept a company from delivering the plane on time, with the promised performance, at a price that allowed the company to make a profit. Aviation companies were particularly prone to these execution problems, because they were delivering so complicated a product, in so regulated an environment, where so many things could go wrong. But they also suffered, Raburn said, because their assembly techniques were at least one technological generation behind those used in the automobile industry, to say nothing of the computer or semiconductor world. And Eclipse, as we will see, had its own ambitious plans to apply these advanced techniques to airplane-building.

These first two assessments might seem to be directed against companies like Cirrus, which after all was chronically underfinanced and which struggled to get all parts of its delivery system working together. But the third element in Raburn's diagnosis of past failures was almost identical to Alan Klapmeier's central claim. Most airplane companies had failed, Raburn said, because most airplane companies did not deserve to succeed.

"The basic reason most companies have failed in aviation is that they didn't offer anything better," Raburn says. "You can ask about any recent product, 'What's different about this airplane?' Is it 2 percent faster? Three percent better? This has been an industry that measured product innovation in single-digit numbers. I came out of a world that measured product innovation in order-of-magnitude changes. And so my first comment to them was, you can't break into a new business—especially a business that's seen as very static, especially a business with products that will kill people if you do something wrong—with a 2 percent improvement. We said, this is an order-of-magnitude change."

How could it be that? This is where Raburn's analysis coincides with those of Bruce Holmes and Dan Goldin and Alan Klapmeier, and all of the others who concluded that the time had come to apply advanced technology to air travel. Computers had brought an order-of-magnitude change, and then some, to the ability to communicate and process information. Raburn claimed that Eclipse would bring a similar change by shifting the value equation between airlines and small planes. Essentially, it would make small airplanes economically attractive again.

"There was a period when general aviation really was a rival to the airlines for *transportation*," as opposed to sheer enthusiast adventure, Raburn says. "You could get close to airline speeds, with something like airline technology. A company could run those planes for the same cost as you could buy tickets on a DC-3. Pretty much through the forties and fifties general aviation was a fair match for the airlines."

The airlines got an edge with the advent of big pressurized airliners like the Constellation, which could fly higher than little planes and therefore get above many weather problems. But the real change came with turbine jet engines. They revolutionized military aviation in the fifties, airliners in the sixties, and big corporate jets by the eighties. Travel in jet-powered airliners was faster, more comfortable, and very much safer than what had been available with piston-powered planes.

"There was this period of economic legitimacy, probably into the sixties, when as a general aviation pilot you could get there as fast and quickly with your own plane," Raburn says. "But then 1978 happened"—airline deregulation. "What really killed general aviation from that point on was not the liability issue. It was that the real competition—not Piper versus Cessna, or Beech versus Mooney, but the airlines—suddenly got a whole lot cheaper. Before 1978, the airlines were more comfortable than little planes, definitely safer, somewhat faster, but not cheaper.

"By 1980, it was a whole lot cheaper. By 1986, People's Express had come and gone, and the airlines had finally figured out: You know, we can sell these two seats, right next to each other, for an order-of-magnitude difference in price on the same flight. I'm in awe of what they figured out through yield management. Once that happened, airlines became finally and definitively cheaper. That put all the nails in the coffin. It wasn't the last nail. It built the coffin and nailed it shut."

Raburn made his pitch for what he said would reverse this: a pocket jet that would really allow people to travel from place to place in ways that avoided the chaos, crowding, and wasted time of the airlines. With Sam Williams's new engines, the company could design a plane that was more comfortable and nearly as safe as modern jetliners, and faster for all but the very longest-haul hub-to-hub trips. There would be no beating a 747 on trips from New York to Tokyo, or even New York to L.A. But the Eclipse 500, as it was eventually called, would be able to travel more than 1,650 miles nonstop, and beat the airlines on most of those routes.

From Chicago, that would mean nonstop travel to any major city in the continental United States except San Francisco.[11]

The passenger zone of the plane would, like the Cirrus, have "automobile-like" comfort. Once again, it demonstrates how far the car business has come since the seventies that "automobile-like" is now a term of praise. The cockpit would have essentially the same displays, information, and controls as those of a modern Boeing jet—and therefore would be simpler to fly than the standard small plane is now. This follows the principle that the more advanced and expensive an airplane is, the simpler and more "Macintosh-like" it seems when you look at the flight controls.

The plane would have a top speed of 368 knots, or 423 miles per hour, and its service ceiling would be 41,000 feet, higher than most airliners actually fly. But it would be designed in such a way that its stall speed—that is, minimum speed at which it would still fly rather than simply falling out of the air—was very low. The lower the stall speed, the slower a pilot can go on the final approach for landing—and the slower the final approach speed, the easier nearly everything about a landing is, since there is more time to make adjustments and the plane is moving more slowly when it actually touches the ground. Moreover, the slower the approach speed, the less distance it takes for the plane to come to a stop after touchdown, so a low stall speed means that an airplane can safely land on short runways. The Eclipse's stall speed, sixty-two knots, would mean a pilot could safely fly at about eighty knots when preparing to land. This is only ten or fifteen knots higher than a slow little Cessna trainer, and is about the same as a Bonanza, a Cirrus, or other fast, small propeller planes. It also means that the Eclipse jet could safely land on runways only 2,500 feet long, which includes most of the small airports in the country. Yet the price for this performance would be far below that of any comparable jet plane on the market. In 1999, when

Raburn was making the road show, a comparable and slower plane from the French company Socata cost $2.3 million. The Cessna CitationJet, slightly faster and with more carrying capacity, but with a much shorter range, cost $3.7 million. The initial target price for the Eclipse 500 was $775,000.

By the time the plane was formally announced, just before the Oshkosh show in 2000, the target price had risen to $837,500. The company promised to honor that price, in 2000 dollars, when the plane went on sale, which it planned for the year 2003. The only adjustment would be for inflation, which is a standard clause in big-ticket capital goods of this sort. "The technology is all here," Raburn would say in wrapping up his pitch. "The execution is all here. We can produce the compelling product. And the market is here. The market is, you don't have to take the airlines!"

Raburn said that when he was trying to raise money for a software company in 1977, he kept getting the same objections from venture capitalists. "'Software?' they'd say. 'Why, the company's assets go out the door every night! Now, a warehouse full of printers, *that's* an investment!'"

Then Lotus went public in 1983, and Microsoft in 1986. "Suddenly it's like, 'Wow! I can invest in software and I don't have to build up inventory!' I actually think that when we succeed, we're going to have the same effect on general aviation that Lotus had on investment in software. Once the financial community sees an opportunity to make money, they are very rational about it."


The first Eclipse 500 will make its first flight on June 17, 2002—or so Vern Raburn said early in 2001. He was slightly joking about the specificity: he expected the plane to be ready a few weeks before that, and to be flying in the summer of 2002 to stay on track for FAA certification that fall, and sales the following year. If the predictions hold—and the plane is ready on schedule, and the FAA approves it without problems, and the company can bring it to market quickly, and enough financing rolls in to meet capital requirements as production rates scale up—then Eclipse may well have leapfrogged competitors to provide the "disruptive technology" that changes the way we travel.

If Raburn, Williams, and their associates succeed in all those ways, how will they have done it? Apart from the engine, and apart from the connections that gave them a start in fundraising, there will have been two essential "new economy" elements in Eclipse's story. One is the use of the computerized design tools that have become common in most parts of the modern industrial economy. The other is the application of advanced manufacturing techniques, including one innovation never before used in the aircraft business.

I had heard Raburn describe the importance of the computerized design tools, but I hadn't really envisioned what he meant until I visited the design team in Walled Lake. The Eclipse corporate offices in Albuquerque had been lightly populated—a few executives, a lot of empty space—but the Walled Lake operation, which took up part of the Williams International headquarters, had the opposite look. The cubicles were filled; people brushed past one another in the corridors; there was more activity than space.

The most immediately noticeable aspect of the activity, however, was that it was all on computers. At one desk, an "aft fuze" engineer—someone working on the portion of the fuselage from wing to tail—was using a program called Unigraphics to consider the shape and placement of a strut. A few feet away, another engineer was simulating the motion of retractable landing gear on his computer screen to make sure that their path of travel was clear of obstructions. At the other end of the room an engineer was looking at a schematic rendering of the plane's interior, and using his computer program to view it from the perspective of passengers in the front seat and then in the back. Stretching for fifty or sixty feet along the office's back wall was a computer-generated project plan, showing when every single component of the plane, from the smallest bolt to the largest wing spar, had to be ready if the plane was to meet its deadlines. The same chart showed exactly how much each piece was allowed to cost and to weigh.

A similar scene would be perfectly normal in the modern automobile business—or at Boeing and Airbus as they planned their newest jets. But the concept of designing and engineering an airplane strictly by computer, rather than building working prototypes and seeing how the parts fit, is a novelty for the GA industry. Oliver Masefield, the Eclipse vice president who was in charge of the Walled Lake team, explained how different the approach was, and its importance for Eclipse.

Masefield, like so many other people in the industry, had "always" been interested in airplanes. He is a tall, muscular man in his early fifties, with aviator-style glasses and a goatee. He grew up in one of England's most prominent aviation families; his father, Sir Peter Masefield, was an influential aircraft designer during World War II, and in the sixties tried to revitalize Britain's small-plane industry with a start-up company called Beagle. (It failed, unable to keep up with American powers like Beech and Cessna.) From the early seventies through the late nineties Masefield had worked at the Swiss aircraft company Pilatus. There he had been responsible for development of the PC-12, a successful turboprop plane. Masefield had dreamed of turning the PC-12 into a jet, equipped with some of Sam Williams's light engines; this brought him into the Williams-Raburn orbit; and in late 1999 he moved from a house overlooking Lake Lucerne to a new sub-division in Walled Lake, to join the Eclipse team.

"Ten or fifteen years ago, when we were planning the PC-12, we built a full-scale metal mock-up," Masefield told me, shortly before showing off Eclipse's computerized design tools. "This was the way to see that the ribs were correct, and the frame was correct, you could fit in all the tubes and pipes. Of course, to get to that metal mock-up you've built jigs, you've built forms, you've built all sorts of things. You've got a lot of money invested in those parts. And if they're wrong, you've got a lot of parts to scrap. The reason for building a metal mock-up is so you can change things. But the financial pressures not to change things are very high."

A full set of computerized design tools, with accompanying workstations and servers, would be even more expensive than the jigs and forms for making the metal mock-up. But, as Masefield said, it would save many times its costs over the years in design flexibility. "It really allows you to optimize your design and not to make compromises you'd normally have to live with. And I discovered that it is much more beneficial to spend more money at the beginning of the program than at the end." The point sounds obvious but is novel or at least enviable in the hand-to-mouth world of small aircraft.

With their investment in computerized design tools, and with the engineers Masefield began recruiting from companies large and small, the Eclipse team began late in 1999 deciding exactly how its first product should differ from the V-Jet II "concept plane" that Burt Rutan had built for Sam Williams.

That there is a family resemblance between the two planes is obvious from looking at them. It is also evident in a more subtle but crucial element of design. In working with Rutan on the V-Jet II, Sam Williams had insisted that the two jet engines be placed

**Mockup of the Eclipse 500.**

together as closely as possible at the rear of the plane. So closely were the engines spaced that if you looked at the V-Jet II from the front, you could not see either engine. The outward sweep of the plane's fuselage blocked both of them from view. This had an intriguing safety advantage for the airplane: it reduced the chance that a "foreign object," most likely a bird, would be sucked into the plane's engines, since the object's inertia as it passed the wide part of the fuselage would take it straight back and away from the engine inlets. It had an even more important implication. If one of the engines failed, the thrust from the other one would be so close to the plane's centerline that the pilot could still keep the plane safely under control.

But in other ways Masefield's team made significant variations. It altered the wing and tail in a variety of ways that reduced the plane's top speed but made it easier to handle, capable of landing on shorter runways, and able to have a larger cabin area. It reconfigured aspects of the cabin itself, with the goal of making it seem like an airborne SUV. And it decided to build the plane out of aluminum, rather than the composites Burt Rutan favored for his design. The reason, once again, was fundamentally about money. If you were planning to build only a few planes, or had limited working capital, composites were the way to go. You set up a few molds, and you could make the parts of your plane. But Masefield argued strongly that for large-scale production, aluminum had clear advantages, as long as a company could face the steep initial costs. For a given degree of strength, it would always be lighter than composites. "But what really kills composites," Masefield told me, "is that the production is so difficult to scale up and automate." Composite materials have to be "cured," or put in an oven for hours and allowed to bake. Time for the curing cycle, even space for the ovens, makes it hard to reach the fast-cycle production Eclipse saw as the key to its profitability.

The design trade-offs were still underway in March 2000, when Raburn first publicly announced that Eclipse existed, and that it was trying to build a small, inexpensive jet. At the Oshkosh air show that summer, Eclipse drew huge crowds to a pavilion in which it displayed a mock-up of the plane's interior. It attracted consistently favorable press, and by the end of the year it had received several hundred deposits for the plane. But the reaction it received to one aspect of the model shown at Oshkosh was more negative than it expected: the plane's projected price and speed sounded great, but the cabin seemed more cramped and submarine-like than many customers expected. Designers went to work on the interior, and were ready to unveil a more spacious-seeming model by the Oshkosh show of 2001.

Meanwhile, the company was also planning to use its financial advantages to invest in novel production techniques. Its biggest gamble was a technology called "friction-stir welding." The sheets of aluminum that make up a plane have to be joined together somehow. The conventional aviation answer is with rivets. But rivets are heavy. They are time-consuming to install. And their installation points inevitably leave imperfections on the plane's surface, which reduce its slipperiness in the air.

So Eclipse decided to embrace friction-stir technology, which had been developed a decade earlier in England. The fundamental idea of this system is to join two pieces of metal by melting them along the border where they meet, and having them congeal as a single, bonded unit. Of course it's more complicated than that, mainly because the "melting" actually involves a kind of plasticizing of the metal, at temperatures below the normal melting point.[12] But the point of the technology is that it provides a connection that is at least as strong as rivets; that makes for a smooth, almost undetectable joint; and that can be done at much higher speeds that riveting can. "With an automatic riveting machine, you can actually set six rivets a minute," Oliver Masefield said in Walled Lake. "Let's say there's a half-inch spacing between the rivets. That's three inches a minute of joint line. Manual riveting is about half that fast. Using friction-stir welding, we're currently running at twenty inches a minute, and we've had very good experience recently at thirty inches a minute. So it's a factor-of-ten increase in jointing speed. For a given volume of production, we can have one machine—versus ten riveting machines. Your investment goes down, your floor space goes down, your cycle time goes up."

The new welding system was a gamble, because the FAA had never before certified it for use in building airplanes. On the mammoth project-planning chart on Eclipse's office wall, March 15, 2001, was listed as the make-or-break date for friction-stir technology. If at that point the new technology still seemed too risky, the company would have switched back to plain old rivets. But the date came and went, and Eclipse put its bets on friction-stir welding.

The company was also studying the "lean manufacturing" techniques pioneered in Japan and adopted in Detroit as a response to the Japanese challenge. These included a version of "just-in-time" supply policies, to reduce the cost of inventory, and an emphasis on parts made to such precise tolerances that they could simply be snapped together on the assembly floor, as the interiors of modern automobiles are. "In the old airplane factories, you see hammers all over the assembly area, and hear people whacking pieces together because they don't exactly fit," Raburn says. "That's because GA has not made the investment in precision equipment like the car makers have. We don't want to see any hammers there."

Through the late months of 2000 and early 2001, I asked Raburn and his colleagues what worried them most about their project. Eclipse had enjoyed great success in recruiting. It had attracted top-line names to work there. The head of sales is Chris Finoff, a deceptively soft-spoken man in his fifties who has sold airplanes all his life and has quickly become the leading salesman in the nation at every company he has worked for. (When we went out for lunch, he turned the tables on me by asking me all about my children, my upbringing, my wife, my interests, before I could start in on him. His instincts as a salesman were quicker than mine as a reporter. Then he picked up the fifteen-dollar tab—"You might be a customer some day!") The director of training is Don Taylor, a United Airlines pilot for thirty years.

Money was the most obvious vulnerability, but through early 2001 the rounds of capital-raising went at least as well as planned. The first two years' worth of production were already sold out. The company had nonrefundable deposits on hand totaling several tens of millions of dollars. It had arranged favorable terms with the city of Albuquerque, similar to Cirrus's deal with Duluth, for tax and rent breaks on the land it would use for its factory there. Eventually the company planned to produce planes "in the four-digit volumes per year," as Raburn puts it, but would build gradually toward those levels until at least 2006.

Weight is the next most obvious problem for every aircraft project. In early 2001, a year and a half before the planned first test flight, the components of the plane added up to 4,950 pounds, rather than the target of 4,700. But Raburn and Masefield claimed that week by week the necessary reductions would work out. A motivational poster on the office wall asked, "What are you going to do *today* to reduce the weight?"

"I think we're just now out of the woods on the scary technical issues," Raburn said early in 2001, just before the go-ahead decision on friction-stir welding. "It should just be a matter of hard work now. What's ahead should be doable. Greatness occurs one step at a time."

The danger to which Eclipse seemed most sensitive, apart of course from the Hindenburg-like catastrophe that can destroy the prospects of any aviation project, was competitive intelligence. In specific terms, Vern Raburn's nightmare was that a sleeping giant, in particular Cessna but perhaps a newcomer like Honda, might notice what was going on and decide to respond. Cessna, after all, was the best-known name in the small-plane business. It had a network of dealers and repair shops around the world. There was no doubt about its competence or staying power. If it showed up at the next trade show saying that it, too, had a new, small jet, priced a few hundred thousand dollars above Eclipse, buyers might think this was a reasonable premium for an established brand.

Therefore Raburn fought his natural volubility and kept mum on crucial business details. He said that his real fantasy for the company had been to operate strictly in "stealth mode," revealing nothing about its plans or existence until it could show up at Oshkosh with several finished, certified airplanes ready for sale. Raburn would never have been able to keep the exciting news to himself that long, and in the real world Eclipse needed publicity in order to attract both capital and talent. But Raburn was under visible torment about the need to bottle up details he would love to share, from order totals to planned production rates. The money that Eclipse is now paying to finish development of the Williams engine means that no one except Eclipse can use that engine for a while. Just how long a while no one is saying, although it is clearly less than five years. "I obviously don't want to lock this thing up forever," Raburn says. "The last thing I want, and this is a direct result of my software experience, is to be the only guy using the thing. I also don't want to create such a huge period of exclusivity that it gives Pratt & Whitney every incentive to develop one on their own. I want everyone else using this same engine—after I've had my head start. I just want my unfair advantage!"

"Whenever I'm on a commercial airplane, I ask the person next to me about their experience," says Peter Reed, Eclipse's head of finance. "Last week I was flying into Philadelphia. The guy next to me said he was a lawyer who had to go to Toledo for the day. I asked him where he lived, and he said about an hour and a half out of town. So he had to get up at 4 A.M. to drive in to the Philadelphia airport, then catch the plane to Detroit, then wait around Detroit Metro for an hour for the connection, then finally get his plane into Toledo. Then at the end of the day, the whole process in reverse.

"I said, 'Is there an airport near where you live?' And he said, 'Yeah, about three miles away.' So I said, 'Here's the deal. If you could have had an airplane pick you up at that airport, fly you to the airport nearest to your client, and then fly you back, for an extra twenty-five to fifty cents a mile on top of what you're paying for coach, would you do it?' And he says, 'In a heartbeat! Bring it on!' I always get that."

This, in essence, is the Eclipse vision. It would be the first company to provide the missing hardware for a new transportation system. This would qualify as "disruptive technology," since it would embody many kinds of change at once: in computerized design, in electronics for the plane itself, in a new kind of engine, in modern techniques of manufacture and assembly. As it became available in the thousands, it would constitute the basis for other industries. In its fund-raising presentations Eclipse estimated that the air-taxi market might amount to 30 million trips a year, within a decade. That would be less than 10 percent of the projected airline total for that time, but it would still mean a fleet of 35,000 small jets. This in turn would mean businesses to schedule the trips, and improved rental-car or normal taxi services at the thousands of small airports that would receive greater traffic. Overnight package delivery, by FedEx and Airborne, changed the way businesses operated in the late twentieth century. Same-day delivery—of perishable goods, of medical supplies or specimens, of anything else with great time value—would be possible with

new, small jets and could change business in the twenty-first century. More than 100,000 corporations in North America had
annual revenues of $10 million or more—or enough to consider
amortizing the cost of a million-dollar plane. (Some 9,000 corporations already have their own planes.) If this market really grew,
Eclipse wouldn't be alone in it: Cirrus might race to join it, Safire
might compete, the giants like Cessna might finally pay attention.
But it would have demonstrated the potential.

"I started feeling back in the early nineties that there would be
some really fascinating opportunities to take these rules and techniques and approaches and apply them to other industries," Vern
Raburn told me in Albuquerque, as we watched the airline traffic
from his office widow. "The new economy is about people, it's
about intellectual property, it's about cycle time. And we're certainly a first derivative of that.

"I absolutely do not believe that in my lifetime we are going to
'virtualize' interpersonal relationships. It's just not going to happen. Videoconferencing, teleconferencing, all that stuff, sure, it's
wonderful. It will be utilized the way copiers, fax machines, e-
mails are utilized. But it is never going to replace sitting down and
breaking bread with one another. Won't replace getting drunk
and pissing on one another's shoes. The human condition does
not fundamentally change.

"Last year was the first year in the history of transportation
when the average speed of travel went down." This might be wrong
in detail; things may well have slowed during the Great Depression
or after the Roman Empire fell. But anyone who has spent time in
airports knows that the general point is right. "It's not supposed to
happen that way. That is a huge, huge, massive disconnect.

"Any time you have a major disconnect in forces in the marketplace, there's an opportunity. That is what our business can be."

# Coast to Coast

A small airplane is not really meant for crossing continents, any more than a car is. If you could average a steady sixty miles per hour in a car, allowing for congestion and places where the enforced speed limit is below sixty, you could make it from the Pacific coast of North America to the Atlantic in forty to fifty hours of driving. If you could average a steady 180 miles per hour in a small plane like the Cirrus, you could do it in fifteen or sixteen hours of flying, with three or four refueling stops. If you were heading east, with the wind at your back, you could cut two or three hours from the flying time. If you were heading west, it could take you several hours more. If speed or convenience were the main factors, as they are for most people on most long-haul trips, you would just get on an airliner and be there in five or six hours.

But sometimes people choose to drive coast-to-coast even when they don't have to, for the experience of seeing what the country is like the entire way. And thus my family had given in to my suggestions that when it came time for our younger son to return from the West Coast to the East before the college year began, we wouldn't just drive him to the San Francisco airport and wave as he got on a plane for Boston. Instead we'd make the trip in a little plane, spending several days together and seeing the continent beneath us as we went. We wouldn't approach this trip as civilians, concerned mainly with efficiency. We would put ourselves in the frame of mind of enthusiasts.

The journey turned out to be just as impractical as a civilian might have suspected, and just as exhilarating as the enthusiast might have hoped. Its realities illustrated how much excitement small planes can offer, and how much they must change before civilians will find them a reasonable option.

I didn't tell many friends about our plans for cross-country travel, because the ones who heard about it tended to act horrified. Maybe it was acceptable for me to indulge a midlife fantasy by learning to fly. If I came to grief, I'd have only myself to blame, and I already had more years behind me than ahead. But to expose my wife, and above all my twenty-year-old son, to the risks of small plane flight seemed impossibly self-indulgent and reckless.

Certain answers had become reassuring to me over the previous few years: that risks were very small as long as the weather was good, that a pilot could avoid the major sources of hazard with careful planning, preflight checking, and a "when in doubt don't go" policy. But I knew these would not convince the average civilian, so I didn't even try. I concentrated on reassuring my family, which had been softened up by my descriptions of the "plane with the parachute" for several years, and on making sure that the conditions actually would be good.

Pilots love the big H's, signifying "high pressure zone," on weather maps of the continent. A high-pressure zone means heavy, cold, dry air pouring down toward the earth's surface from the upper reaches of the atmosphere. It drives clouds away; it lets you see for miles; it generally creates the circumstances that are best for flight. As we prepared for the trip the map showed a giant H across the whole western half of the United States.

The plane itself was less than a year old, and had recently had a full inspection. Its cabin, apart from being comfortable, was full of the Klapmeiers' moving maps, which would make it hard to lose our way. And there was no denying the comforting effect of the parachute. There should be no problem going over the Rockies, there should be no problem on long stretches at night. But if there were, with my wife and son on board, I didn't mind knowing that there was a handle at the top of the cabin to pull, if it came to that.

There were risks; but they seemed well within reason. And so, after I had done the routine equipment checks and tests on the engine, after I'd opened all the maps and punched in the destination—next stop, Salt Lake City—into the plane's navigation devices, I told the tower at the Oakland airport, "Cirrus One-One-Niner Charlie Delta, ready for departure to the east."

We were cleared for takeoff; we turned out onto a runway that pointed more or less toward Salt Lake City, and with a final check of doors, seat belts, and safety gear I pushed the throttle all the way forward and the plane started to roll. When its airspeed indicator showed that it was going seventy knots, just over eighty miles an hour, I started pulling back gently on the control stick to move the plane's nose up above the horizon. Slowly we could feel the weight coming off the wheels. One hundred feet above the ground; five hundred; a thousand. Then a turn to the right, a little farther toward the east. My family looked down on the Berkeley Hills, rising beneath us. As we came over their crest we saw the vast Central Valley, full of farms. On the other side were the Sierra

Nevada mountains, and on the other side of that, the rest of the country. We were on the way.

In aviation as in many other things, the United States seems a collection of countries. Pilots in the South spend half the year worried about thunderstorms, which practically never occur along the Pacific coast. Pilots in Seattle spend November through March worrying that the perpetual layer of cloud will be cold enough to be full of ice. Pilots in the desert Southwest go months without seeing cloudy skies. But they know that on sunny afternoons, the sand can be baked to temperatures well over 120 degrees, producing the rapidly rising "thermal" columns that can lift, jostle, and upset any plane that flies through them. And pilots headed east, from the West Coast, as we were, know that "high terrain," otherwise known as mountains, will dominate their attention through the first part of the trip.

From the San Francisco Bay, the mountains begin gently. As we turned east, following the Sacramento River toward the interior, the Berkeley Hills were to our right, the Napa Valley to our left. A more chic setting than this would be hard to imagine. Another predictable surprise of small-plane flight is how compact urban areas are—the Midwest or Great Plains region might seem to stretch on forever, but in just a few minutes you can go from one part of a city to another that you're used to thinking of as remote. So it was here: barely five minutes after we had left the University of California–Berkeley campus behind us, we had the farming land of California's Central Valley in view. Starting with family car trips through this area when I was a child, I had learned to think of its various components as distinct entities, each with a characteristic look and tone, and each clearly separate from the others. The Central Valley, now below me, was hot and dusty, with agricultural trucks rattling along the highways. The Napa Valley had its obviously different culture and connotations—but while flying I could still see it, just off the left wing. On the eastern side of the valley, in the Sierra Nevada foothills, were the remains of the old Gold Rush settlements. To go there by car was to feel the air cooling after the long drive across the flat valley. In the airplane, we could see how close mining sites like Placerville actually were to the farming towns. And straight ahead, as we climbed more steeply, the Sierra Nevada slopes themselves. Highly developed skiing resorts, to our left, on the south shore of Lake Tahoe. The far shore of the lake was ringed with more development, because of the casinos on the Nevada side of the border. Off our right wing, a different, wilder, more arid kind of mountain terrain, as we looked toward Yosemite. I had the plane in a steady climb, because straight ahead was the main ridge of the Sierra Nevada range.

It was at this point that a civilian/enthusiast divide began to emerge in the cozy cabin of our plane. I was the one enthusiast aboard, and my concerns about the Sierra Nevada mountains were mainly about our plan for crossing them. I had picked out the Donner Pass on my map, the lowest point on a course more or less straight east from the San Francisco Bay. I realized that the name of the pass might not be reassuring, because of the pioneer party that had been stranded there and turned to cannibalism. But it was the safest and most efficient route.

For the civilians the pass marked the first of a series of disappointing surprises through the day. We had to climb to nearly 10,000 feet to get over the mountains. As we did, I mentioned that my wife and son might want to start looking at their fingernails, to make sure they weren't turning blue. Legally we didn't need to start using supplemental oxygen until we reached 12,500 feet, and then only if we were at that altitude for more than thirty minutes. But there was no harm in checking the first physical sign of oxygen shortage, which was a blue tint in the nail beds. This had the same calming effect as a lifeguard saying, "We're not expecting many sharks today." Nervous glances were exchanged between my wife and son.

Then, as we went through the Donner Pass with Sierra crests on either side, I had the opportunity to begin the catalogue of the different kinds of turbulence we were likely to go through. Oh, the bumps we're feeling right now, as we near the mountain? As if we were on a sled going down a very rough hill? That's mountain turbulence. It's what happens when the wind is coming over the hills and gets disrupted into swirls and eddies. Nothing to worry about!

Half an hour later, the mountains and their mountain waves were behind us, and the vast high desert of Nevada was ahead. Oh, those bumps we're feeling now, as if someone were pulling us up and down on a string? Those are thermals, the columns of hot air rising from the blast-furnace surface of the desert. Nothing to worry about! And you wouldn't believe how much stronger they would be in a normal rental plane! Why, the design of this plane, with its "high wing loading," really damps down the bumps.... But I think I was losing their attention.

The moving map in the front of the plane provided a clear picture of how far we'd come—and how many miles across the desert west we still had to go. I could sense my family's attention riveted on one part of the display, which was the number of minutes left till arrival at our destination. Our first planned stop was Salt Lake City, and as we got well into the "thermal" zone, the meter showed more than two hours left. Things got quiet in the cockpit. Later my wife and son said that as the thermals went on they were thinking: Can we stand two more *hours* of this?

I made sure they could see the air-sickness bags I'd filched over the months whenever taking a commercial airline trip, but through force of will they held off. I often got carsick as a child and have never thought I have a cast-iron stomach, but I felt fine. The person actually flying the plane rarely becomes airsick, even in conditions that makes everyone else groan. Probably this is because, in an airplane as in a car, being at the controls increases one's sense of having some influence over events, rather than just being an object. While we're on the subject: I have felt sick enough to vomit only twice in several hundred small-plane flights, in each case when I knew that the instructor sitting next to me was really in charge. Once was the first time I flew in turbulence "under the hood," with a device that kept me from seeing outside the plane and therefore forced me to concentrate on the instrument panel. The other was the first time I did "spin training"—deliberately putting the plane into, well, nauseating nose-first descents, so as to learn how to get out of them.

But things got better! The thermals abated. The flat desert turned into mountains. We climbed a little higher, our fingernails stayed nice and pink, and I found a way to divert attention from the countdown clock. One solution was to attach a CD player to the plane's intercom. My wife is a devotee of Enya's music, and Enya is at her best when accompanying a trip through the skies. The more engrossing distraction was outside the airplane, for as we moved from Nevada toward Utah, there was the sort of display of spires, canyons, grottoes, mesas, and formations that makes even the queasy civilian stare rapt.

Salt Lake City International was the one major hub airport we tried to land at on this journey, and was a reminder of why such landings are a bad idea. The approach was surreal in its lunar beauty: first the vast whiteness of the Bonneville Salt Flats, then the expanse of the Great Salt Lake, then a sharp right turn around some cliffs to see the airport ahead of us—and then, to my dismay, an assigned place in the landing sequence behind one Delta jet and ahead of another. To avoid delaying the big boys, the controller kept telling me, "Keep speed up, keep speed up" on the approach. The faster the approach speed, the less the margin for error on landing, very much like heading into a parking space at forty miles per hour. I had been in conditions sort of like this many times before. In Seattle, I had flown in and out of Boeing Field, just a few miles from Seattle-Tacoma International. There I had waited my turn on the runway or on the approach path behind 757s, 737s, and on one memorable occasion a B-1 bomber. At Salt Lake City, the controller was trying to squeeze me in faster than I was ready. When he said, "Make short approach," which is more or less like doing a U-turn and diving for the ground, I was simply going too fast to touch down and stop safely before the end of the runway. So I had to "go around"—pour on the gas and take off again before ever having landed, in order to circle for another approach. This was embarrassing, in front of the controller and in front of my family. While not in itself actively dangerous it is clearly undesirable at a busy field. When we finally did get down and had taxied over to the GA side of the field, we recalled the good side of the GA travel style: tips from the locals about where we could get a good lunch, free use of the "crew car" to drive out to the restaurant. But, I told myself, this was nuts. No more competition with 737s on landing. Next time through Utah, a stop at the nearby Ogden or Brigham City airports.

Salt Lake City had one more surprise challenge as we left. The enemies of airplane performance are the "Three H's"—conditions that are high, hot, and humid. (These are not to be confused with the good "H," the welcome high-pressure system on the weather map.) The denser the air is, the better every part of the plane works. There are more molecules of oxygen in each engine cylinder to create power at combustion time; there are more molecules for the propeller to work against as it cuts through the air; there are more molecules flowing over and pushing against the wing to hold up the plane. The hotter the air, the higher the altitude, and the greater the relative humidity, the thinner the air will be, and the worse the plane will fly. (Humidity matters because the relative density of water vapor is less than that of air.)

Salt Lake City was far from humid, but it was high, and the air was extremely hot. The outside temperature was over 100° Fahrenheit at takeoff time, and immediately to our west was a 10,000-foot mountain range. Essentially this was the moment on our trip when we were crossing the continental divide. On the long, airliner-scale runway at Salt Lake City, I pushed in the throttle and kept watching the airspeed indicator, waiting for the plane to gain enough speed to begin to lift off. Airspeed, too, is affected by heat, humidity, and altitude. Airspeed is measured by the pressure of the air on a little device known as the "pitot tube," mounted on the wing. The thinner the air, the fewer molecules there are to bump into and be measured by the sensors in the pitot tube. At a very high airport, you could be going seventy-five knots down the runway, yet the tube could show a speed ten to fifteen knots less. No matter what the altitude, the plane requires the same airspeed before it will lift off, about seventy knots in the case of the Cirrus. This makes sense, because the same air pressure that is hitting the little tube is what is supporting the wings.

After what seemed an agonizing time of hurtling down the runway but was probably only a matter of seconds, the airspeed indicator came alive. Fifty knots, sixty, up to seventy—and it was time to climb. We headed back over the lake again, to circle and gain altitude for the push across the nearby mountains. Then we were at the crest, at 11,500 feet with a thousand feet of air beneath us, looking right down on the crags of the Wasatch Range. Eastward now, toward land that was already in twilight, toward Wyoming. Laramie? Cheyenne? In one or another of these places we hoped to spend the night.

As my wife and son and I left Salt Lake City on the first afternoon of our cross-country trip in a Cirrus SR20, we were ready for another adventure, that of a night flight across the mountain west. Unlike racing the "empty" reading on the gas tank, racing the sun should not be dangerous in itself. Flying at night is in many ways exhilarating, for civilian passengers and enthusiasts alike. The air is usually calmer than in the day. Nighttime thermals do not exist. On clear nights the lights of distant cities are visible from fifty miles away. The lights of other planes stand out far more vividly at night, which gives a strange sense of community.

But nighttime has its problems too. You often can't see clouds, and can fly into them by mistake. Statistically the most dangerous phase of flight is "night IMC"—that is, sustained flight inside the clouds in the dark. In principle it should be no more dangerous to fly a plane strictly by watching the instruments at nighttime than in the day. In each case, the idea is that the gauges and gyroscopes replace the outside perspective that the clouds have blocked from view. But in reality there are far more accidents per instrument flying hour in the dark than in the light.

There weren't any clouds to worry about—the giant-H high-pressure system had turned the sky over the whole western half of the country blue. But there were mountains, great big ones, and unlike high towers or other hazards they didn't have warning lights on top. So as the light faded behind us, I kept edging the plane higher and higher, for an extra-large cushion of safety over the peaks of the Medicine Bow range.

The light lasted long enough for us to marvel at the remoteness of the mountain west settlements. Part of our route paralleled Interstate 80, which was filled with long-distance trucks. We had a good tailwind and were moving about three times as fast as the traffic on the ground. We would see a long gash across the Wyoming range land, site of a huge strip mine. On one side of the gash, the shopping-center-sized dredge that dug it out. A mile or two away, the mobile homes of the people working the mine. The aeronautical maps for metropolitan areas barely have room to list the cities you're flying over. The "Cheyenne Sectional" map we were using was so short on human settlements that it noted the appearance of landmarks like "ranch," "building," "lumber mill" on the ground.

A straight-line course to the two cities we were aiming for, Laramie and Cheyenne, would have taken us across the very highest mountains of the area, at 12,000 feet and more. So we did an arc to the north, over slightly lower ranges, and in full darkness neared what would be the last ridge of mountains on the trip. I knew there was a line of 9,000-foot mountains straight ahead of us. But I knew it from the map on my lap, illuminated by a cabin light, and by the "moving map" display on the Cirrus's dashboard, which showed the elevations that were ahead of us, I couldn't see a thing: the place where the mountains were was just an extra-black part of the scenery ahead, with no starlight from the sky and none of the cabin or road lights we would occasionally glimpse below.

The plane was flying at 11,500 feet, which should be plenty of room. The night wind was flat, dead calm. The passengers were beginning to sense that the aerial tour could be pleasant, not just endurable. The maps, the charts, the indications said that everything would be fine. Still I was relieved at the moment when we crossed over the ridge—and knew we had done so by suddenly seeing the lights of Cheyenne twenty miles away.

After we landed at the airport, we heard that we had just missed the excitement. A big Delta jet had made an emergency landing. A fire had been reported on board, and while it proved to be a false alarm, a planeload of passengers was going to spend the night in Cheyenne rather than where they'd thought they would end up, which we were told was Detroit. To them, the Cheyenne airport must have represented the podunk wastelands. To us, it looked like civilization.

It represented something else to us, too, which was the end of the West. Behind us was a day of mountain ranges and flight altitudes just below where we would have needed to use oxygen. When we left the next morning, in what had become a strong wind, we had ahead of us essentially 1,500 miles of gentle down slope.

The first time I'd been in a small plane on a cross-country trip, I'd seen a reminder of this east-west division, and on leaving Cheyenne we took a brief side trip so I could show my family too. Cheyenne is near the eastern edge of Wyoming; with a few minutes flight east, we were in Nebraska. And with a few minutes more to the north, we were over the city and the geological feature both named Scotts Bluff. Conceptually Cheyenne might be the border of the mountain West, but Scotts Bluff makes the difference dramatic. On the west side of the town is a steep escarpment, running north-south. One isolated, mesalike structure is what pioneers knew as Scotts Bluff, but the whole range gives a sense of being the imposing start of the western mountain lands. On the other side, the land is abruptly flat, as if its soil had been laid down in sedimentary processes rather than raised up violently through the collision of the earth's plates. As we passed over Scotts Bluff and headed east, the land as far ahead as we could see was like the surface of the ocean, level and limitless.

The roads started to become straight, rather than twisting through mountain passes. There weren't farms yet—it was too dry—but there were ranches, with herds of cattle that occasionally looked up as we passed. It was safe to go lower now and improve the view. I kept descending slowly as we went over grasslands marked on the charts as migratory bird reserves, when I saw a reason not to go down any more. From our left—the north, as we headed toward the Atlantic—the sky was suddenly full of great pulsating white clouds. These were flocks of birds, heading south in the fall. If these were geese or ducks, they'd given up the classic V-shaped migratory formation. They were in pulsing balls, like schools of fish, and each ball seemed to contain thousands of birds. They were perhaps 1,000 feet below us, and that was as close as I wanted to be. A "bird strike" in a little plane is no laughing matter, and not just for the birds. Large birds, as these seemed to be, can break the windshield or canopy of a plane as they collide at over 150 miles an hour.

Day one: leaving Oakland.

I edged the plane up, farther away from the birds, and gave the controller a report—"Numerous flocks of large white birds, appear to be migrating, approximately 5,000 feet." The controller asked me which way they were heading. I couldn't tell if he was being sarcastic or sincerely asking for information, so I didn't say "Duh" after saying "Southbound." For the last hour, the air-traffic control frequencies had been basically silent, as they usually are away from the cities. Suddenly they came to life, with other pilots chiming in to ask details of the bird sightings, or to report what they had seen. It was like the scenes in Tarzan movies when the silent jungle comes to life as an intruder is detected.

The miles went on. The roads became straighter and more closely spaced. The vegetation was greener. The first farms appeared. We had reached Iowa. With each passing mile, it was as if we were watching a speeded-up video of the civilizing process. Where there were isolated ranch houses, there became clusters of buildings around an intersection. Then small settlements. Then tidy villages, with school buses wending down the streets in what might have been the first day of school. Soon we were seeing almost ridiculously perfect bits of Americana out the windows: the county courthouse, the church, the schoolyard, and the houses with gardens in back and white fences in front.

We needed gas, and we had picked out our landing spot— Ames, in the middle of Iowa. In the hour before we neared the airport, the ride had become surprisingly bumpy, and as I got ready to land, I understood why. A new kind of turbulence to explain! A very strong wind had the windsock at the airport standing straight out. Fortunately the gale, as I was coming to think of it, was aligned directly with the runway, not at a bothersome cross-angle. But as we landed and tied down the plane, we saw the cause of the wind: what looked like a wall of big thunderheads on the eastern horizon, just where we planned to go.

It was only early afternoon, but the choice was easy. We would spend the night in Ames, and watch TV reports about the local Iowa State Cyclones preparing for their big game that weekend, against arch-rival Iowa.

After our night in Ames, the line of storms had blown through—or so the weather briefers told us. We had half the country still to cross, and wanted to do it in a day. So we zoomed toward Lansing, Michigan, to refuel and get food at the Capitol City Airport. The landscape beneath was becoming ever more settled, with the first signs of small industries. But we had a harder and harder time seeing it, because a layer of cloud was thickening beneath us. The layer rose slowly until it was barely a thousand feet below us. We would need to penetrate it to land at Lansing, so I received a clearance to fly the rest of the trip as an instrument flight plan. The civilians had their first taste of what the most experienced pilot must still find thrilling: we descended through the clouds, guided by the indications on the instrument panel, and then, 1,500 feet above the ground, broke out of the clouds to see the landscape beneath us and the main runway of Lansing's airport straight ahead.

We trekked from the general aviation buildings at Lansing to its "real" airport, where we went through the metal detectors and found a restaurant for lunch. Conditions seemed right to make it to Boston by the end of the day. The wind was at our backs. The storm we'd worried about yesterday was said to be moving south. The radar scopes seemed to show a clear path to the north of it, edging Lakes Erie and Ontario and on through upstate New York. Distances east of the Mississippi seemed puny in any case—we could knock off several states in the time it had taken to get across Nevada—and so we headed off.

The sights-to-see were more densely packed now. Familiar

eastern names and landmarks coming one by one. Because we were moving in and out of clouds and were on an instrument flight plan, I had to ask permission to circle for a few minutes over Niagara Falls, wingtip pointing straight down into the cataract as we stared at it from a few thousand feet up. One of my son's friends was attending college in London, Ontario. We circled above the dorms there, too, trying to pick out which one was hers. The civilians were enjoying this, getting a God's-eye perspective on familiar terrain. They enjoyed it until the trip's last and most serious lesson in turbulence.

I'd watched the weather channel obsessively the night before and early that morning in Ames, and had spent long sessions on the phone with the weather briefer, all in an attempt to find out where the big thunderstorm we'd met in Iowa was headed next. All the evidence seemed to be that it was heading south. The farther north we went, the better our chances of staying out of its way. After deliberating with the weather briefer, I filed a flight plan that seemed to do the job. There should be fifty miles or more between us and the nearest "convective activity," as thunderstorms are called. Or so it appeared when we took off.

As we kept going north, though, the storm neglected to move south. With the controllers' advice, we went more northward still—along the southern shore of Lake Ontario, then far up through northern New York, toward Quebec. Still the distance between us and the storm seemed to diminish. I was following it on a "storm scope" on the instrument panel, showing the distance and location of nearby lightning strikes. The prevailing winds that had been driving the storm south had either stalled or reversed, and the storm was coming back our way.

Air-traffic controllers seem at their best when the situation is at its worst, and we were in the care of a very good one. For reasons I've never heard explained, the controllers at military air fields are gentler-sounding and more personable than the average one in the civilian system. As we tried to find the right way around the storm, we were talking to a controller from the Wheeler-Sack army airfield at Fort Drum, in the far northern tip of New York. On his radar screen, he could see where we were, and where the storm was going. Officially controllers are not responsible for giving weather advice, but unofficially he said, "Looks to me like your best bet is to go straight through." There was a break in the storm, he said, that we could get through in five to ten minutes.

And so we did. For five or six of those minutes, I was taken back to the time of early solos, trying to match my intellectual understanding that everything should be fine with my emotional desire to be out of this situation. I brought the plane back to its "maneuvering speed," slower than top speed, to avoid too much strain on the structure if it hit a bad bump. I concentrated strictly on the instruments, since there was nothing but cloud to see outside, and just tried to keep the plane pointed in the right direction as it

Day two: leaving Cheyenne.

bounced up and down. I watched the storm scope, to keep heading away from the lightning zone. Planes are designed to absorb lightning strikes, but you'd rather not prove the point. "How ya' doin' up there?" the controller asked at one point. "Continuous moderate turbulence," I replied. Ah, "moderate" turbulence again, from the Chuck Yeager school of understatement. The plane was never out of control, which is when "severe" turbulence begins.

At the time my wife found comfort in the controller's solicitude. Later she was upset in thinking about why he might have been sounding so gentle. I tried to keep up a jaunty patter for the benefit of the passengers. I was jaunty because I knew, with my left brain, that the situation was not dire. The plane was designed to stand far worse than this. We were 10,000 feet above the ground and had a lot of room to recover if anything went wrong. I'd trained again and again in pulling airplanes out of spins and stalls. The lightning should pose no dire threat. And there was ... the parachute.

But we all wanted it to be over. If we'd seen it coming, or if the weather briefers had thought the storm would reverse its course, we could have gone far north into Canada or far to the south. But in ten minutes, it was over. And somewhere over southern New Hampshire, we broke out of the clouds. Before us was a calm, sunny, poststorm New England day, under a high blue sky. My wife put on Enya once again. We began our descent to Hanscom Field, in Bedford, a dozen miles west of Boston. In the clear air before us we saw the skyline of Boston, the crooked arm of Cape Cod, the Atlantic in the sun.

"Bedford Tower, this is Cirrus One-One-Niner Charlie Delta. Inbound for landing." We'd come to the end.

For the enthusiast, it all qualified as an adventure. Lots of scenery, lots of weather, lots of challenges, lots of things seen and learned.

It was like crossing the ocean in a sailboat, something whose justification was the experience itself.

The enthusiast side of the adventure had a few more days to run. The plane had to get back to its home, in Duluth. After dropping off our son in Boston, my wife and I returned to Hanscom Field and made a thirty-five minute, low-altitude flight to New Haven. It was a startlingly different view of a part of New England I'd seen from turnpike-level countless times. The cities seemed almost to disappear into the vast forests. The white steeples of village churches were like signals marking the way. New Haven's Tweed Airport, on the Long Island Sound, had a kind of seascape magnificence. In New Haven my wife got onto the train to New York, for several days of meetings. My friend Linc Caplan took her place in the plane. Together we made the last day's journey back to the Midwest.

It was a recapitulation of the grandeur and the inconvenience of the three-day journey eastward. In the first hour out of New Haven, we crossed the suburbs and shopping malls of greater New York and soon were in corduroy-like coal country of Pennsylvania. The clouds had been thin, but they began to increase, and (on an instrument flight plan) we had the vertiginous experience of roaring into clouds and bursting out a second later. When the plane is in clear skies it is easy to forget how fast it's going; cutting in and out of ragged cloud layers makes its speed dramatic. Linc put a CD into the player. By chance the song that came on was a jazz guitar version of "Come Fly with Me."

The clouds become thicker and darker outside Cleveland. Soon we were bumping around unpleasantly. "Continuous moderate," I had to tell the controller once again, when asking for permission to head for calmer air. The clouds parted; we saw the Lake Erie shoreline to our right; straight ahead was the Toledo airport, where we would fuel the plane (and "defuel" ourselves, as the pilots' euphemism goes, after nearly four hours of sitting in the plane and sipping water and coffee). In Toledo the weather briefers told me that there'd be no more turbulence or trouble between there and Minnesota. This time they were right. In glassy conditions we passed over South Bend, Indiana, seeing the golden dome of Notre Dame; across part of the lake, seeing Chicago's skyline in the sun; and then, with the sun setting in front of us, the small, scalloped lakes dotting the woods of the upper Midwest.

We planned to spend the night in the Twin Cities area, so that Linc, an enthusiast at heart, could take an airline flight back home the next day, while I took the plane to Duluth. In the twilight sky over the city, we saw a dozen sets of lights, from the big planes lining up to land at Minneapolis–St. Paul International. We were headed instead to the downtown St. Paul airport, a field on the banks of the Mississippi, a five-minute cab ride from the main hotels of St. Paul. We landed, parked the plane, and celebrated the end of the adventure in a brew pub.

From the civilian perspective, crossing the continent in a small plane is undeniably odd. My wife and son said they were glad to have had the experience, but half the time they were clearly thinking: What have we done? To be effective for really long flights, planes would have to be a lot faster than today's propeller planes. They would have to be able to fly above or around the weather. They would, in short, have to be jets.

But for journeys less than the full coast-to-coast haul, even planes like the Cirrus could make the case for themselves. Linc Caplan and I left New Haven just before noon and were in St. Paul for a late dinner. It took him far longer to get back, by hub-and-spoke routing on jets. The trip from Boston to New Haven was the easiest, fastest, and most pleasant way in which I have ever covered those one-hundred-plus miles. On modest-length trips along the East and West coasts I have used small planes to get where I was going faster than I could in any other way. Seattle to Portland. The Washington, D.C., suburbs to the suburbs of Philadelphia or Boston. Oakland to inland southern California, to visit my parents. Vancouver to Seattle. The San Francisco area to Lake Tahoe, less than an hour, or to Sedona and the Grand Canyon, four hours in a little plane versus at least twice that by any other means. Each of these trips has required careful checks of the weather. Each has demanded my full attention during the flight, which in fact I regarded as a plus. But each began and ended on the schedule I chose, not the one I'd planned three weeks earlier with the airlines.

With nicer small planes like the Cirrus, it seems reasonable that more people would become enthusiasts. With nice, fast, safe, small jets like the one Eclipse has promised, it seems certain that many more civilians would welcome an alternative to the airlines. The equipment that can make that alternative a reality is in prospect. Let us, finally, consider how it might look and what it might mean.

# Epilogue: Free Flight

As business stories, Cirrus and Eclipse are both admirable—no, inspiring. The more I have learned about the obstacles they face, the more impressed I have become by their daring in thinking they could actually design, deliver, and produce new airplanes.

Cirrus has survived on talent, daring, family money, and family stubbornness. If the brothers had simply been businessmen, not aviation enthusiasts who were also entrepreneurs, they would likely have increased their family's holdings more easily in some other way. Depending on how they manage the perilous process of rapid growth with limited funds, they have a chance to establish a real business success. Even if Cirrus proves, in the long run, to have been beaten by what the Klapmeiers consider the "irrationality" of financial markets, it has already achieved something significant. With appropriate allowances, it can call itself the Apple of the airplane industry. It presented a new design and personality for its products. It created a cadre of enthusiasts who thought it had shown a new future for the industry as a whole.

Eclipse's immediate aim is even bigger. If its plans are fulfilled, it has a chance to change daily life not just for its admirers, not just for enthusiasts fascinated by new ways to fly, but for the whole of the traveling public. These judgments must be conditional, of course, until its products hit the market in 2003.

And what the federal government has accomplished, through the efforts of Dan Goldin, Bruce Holmes, and their colleagues in NASA, is in a sense the most surprising part of the story. It is certainly the one to have received least public note or acclaim. Starting more than a decade ago, senior officials in NASA saw today's airline morass impending. With cumulative expenditures of some $180 million, or less than sevety cents per American, they encouraged competition among private companies to design the engines, wings, guidance systems, and safety protections that could make small-plane aviation a more realistic alternative for civilian travel.

The people who have achieved these things are themselves all enthusiasts. Bruce Holmes, for one, takes the view that the enthusiast population will grow significantly in the long run. It's not worth asking whether more of today's middle-aged men and women will be drawn to flying, he says. The people to watch are now ten years old. "If you went back to the time of the Wright Brothers and asked if the average person would travel on an airplane, the answer would be, You've got to be kidding. Over time that changes." It changed because airline travel became safer, cheaper, ubiquitous, routine. Personal air travel—that is, people flying their own aircraft—can change in the same way, he says, provided that small airplanes become safer, cheaper, ubiquitous, routine. Toward that end NASA has launched numerous other programs under its Small Aircraft Transportation System, or SATS, to make flying a plane as close as possible to driving a car.[1] For instance, pilots could easily see when to climb, turn, descend, or avoid hazards by following computer-generated "highway in the sky" displays, even if it were pitch dark or cloudy outside the plane.

Suppose that a generation from now planes have become safer, cheaper, simpler to operate, more comfortable, according to all the targets NASA has set out. "Then the traveler will have the choice of standing in line for the ever more crowded hub-and-spoke system, or transporting himself," Holmes says. "She could drive ten minutes to the local airport, get to her destination two or three times faster than on the airlines, and find a rental car waiting on the other end. If the prognosticators are right, and the 'golden rule' is 'time is gold,' cultural adaptation will lead us this way."

Between that hope and today's reality lie numerous practical challenges. Above all, small-plane flight must become much safer. Turbine engines are the main step in this direction. The fatal-accident rate for airlines fell by 90 percent from the forties, when planes mainly had piston engines, to the eighties, when they were nearly all jets. The engines weren't the only factor, but they were the most important. Their effect should be similar in small planes. Better navigation systems, better anti-icing systems, more durable cabins, parachutes, and other innovations should make a difference too. Sooner or later, what Bruce Holmes calls the "Airborne Internet" will become a reality. This involves wireless broadband transmissions, which would give every pilot immediate access to information about hazardous weather, oncoming traffic, and other conditions that can make the difference between a safe and unsafe flight.

Small planes must become cheaper. In their different ways, Cirrus and Eclipse are demonstrating progress in that direction. The techniques that have driven down cost and driven up quality for cars, computers, appliances, and most other products will eventually reach the aircraft business too.

New small planes are much simpler to operate than old ones, but they can become much simpler still. In the fifties, futurologists routinely predicted that cars would soon be able to guide themselves along freeways. The driver would punch in a destination, and the car would do the rest. It hasn't worked for land travel, and won't for a long time—but the airborne equivalent of such a system is almost in place right now. The autopilot and GPS-guidance systems aboard the humble Cirrus are already capable of guiding the plane through virtually every phase of the flight. If I wanted, I could turn on the Cirrus's autopilot a few seconds after takeoff, enter my destination and the exact route I'd like to follow, and not worry about the controls until the plane was 300 feet above the runway at its destination, on the proper glideslope for landing.

A full "free flight" system,[2] which is the FAA's term for letting the computer in each plane find its own most direct route across the sky, requires more power than the Cirrus has aboard. Ultimately each plane must be able to detect all others in the vicinity, adjust its path for weather problems or high terrain, and synchronize its planned arrival at the destination for smooth sequencing with others going to the same place. But this is the sort of task at which computers excel. The challenge of routing planes through

Computer-generated "Synthetic vision" lets the pilot "see" his destination, even if the real view is obscured by dark or clouds.

the sky is conceptually like that of routing data packets across the Internet. Garrett Gruener is a veteran pilot and a computer entrepreneur who cofounded the Internet search engine company Ask Jeeves. He says, in principle such a system could leave the pilot with only two controls. One would be "Go," beginning the process of steering the plane to its destination. The other would be "Trouble," a failsafe device, like the Cirrus parachute, to rely on if things went wrong.

Then there is the challenge of airports. It is difficult to imagine modern America building more of them, but the vast majority of those already built are mostly idle most of the time. Twenty airports in the country can barely accommodate another flight. Four thousand other airports could handle, on average, ten times the traffic they now receive. This would mean more noise at smaller airports, which is why progress toward much quieter engines is another "must do" on NASA's list. But it would mean less noise at big airports too. The noise burden rises heavily with the size of the plane. Twenty planes, each carrying five people, can with the right engines have a smaller total noise "footprint" than a single airliner carrying one hundred people. The tiny Williams jet engine, built for the Eclipse, is much more powerful than a standard propeller engine, and much quieter too.

"A lot of the noise issue is perceptual," Bruce Holmes says. He means not that it's purely subjective but that society tolerates nuisances differently, depending on the value they may create. A generation from now, participation in the national small-aircraft network could make the difference between regions that develop economically and regions that stagnate. "How will the person who's now fifteen years old feel, when he's grown up, if the airport is what keeps his city from being a backwater?" Holmes asks. "How will people come to perceive the value of on-demand, direct access, at jet speeds, to wherever they need to go?" Holmes's own answer is that human beings have shown they value access and opportunity highly, and will welcome the sound of incoming small jets as country folk used to welcome the whistle of the arriving train.

An expanded small-plane fleet would also use more fossil fuel. No small plane can carry as many people, as far, as fast, on a gallon of fuel as a 747 can. Similarly, no automobile can match a train in fuel efficiency. But cars still have their place, and car engines can be made much more efficient—as they are when the price of oil rises significantly. Similar progress is possible with aviation engines. Already, many small planes compare favorably with cars. The Cirrus gets about twenty miles to the gallon, carrying four people, but at two to three times the speed of a car. Moreover, the pure efficiency of airline travel needs to be adjusted for all the inefficiencies it creates. The congestion to and from the airport, the fleets of buses to car-rental stands and satellite lots, all the overhead that comes with a crowded, centralized system.

The big airlines will, naturally, play the leading part in the high-speed transportation. They will be the way to go from New York to Los Angeles, from Atlanta to Seattle, from Washington to London, and on any long-haul routes. But they obviously need help doing the job. They have reached the limits of what the system can handle and the passenger can endure. When the help arrives, and citizens can visit their relatives without trekking hours ahead of time to the airport, and salesmen can go from one small city to the next without endless routing through the crowded hubs, and hospitals can get specimens and supplies from the other end of the country in the same day, and a family in Los Angeles doesn't have to cancel its trip to Kansas City because there was snow in Denver—when these things happen, civilians should give a thought to the enthusiasts whose efforts and obsession made a better system real.

# Notes

## Introduction

1. Daniel S. Goldin, keynote address, Aircraft Owners and Pilots Association convention, Palm Springs, Calif., October 24, 1998.
2. More than 4,000 airports in the United States have paved runways at least 3,000 feet long, which generally is enough for GA airplanes. Nearly 1,700 have runways at least 5,000 feet long. There are active control towers at 523 airports. More than 600 have "precision approaches," which allow planes to land safely even with low clouds.
3. Bruce J. Holmes, "Life After Airliners IV," EAA AirVenture 2000, Oshkosh, Wisconsin, July 29, 2000.
4. Melanie Trottman, "Tired of Waiting, Stranded Fliers Try Unusual Ways to Alleviate Airport Rage," *Wall Street Journal*, August 14, 2000.
5. Malcolm MacPherson, *The Black Box: All-New Cockpit Voice Recorder Accounts of In-Flight Accidents* (New York: Morrow, 1998).
6. Laurence Zuckerman and Matthew L. Wald, "Crisis for Air Traffic System: More Passengers, More Delays," *New York Times*, September 5, 2000.

## Chapter 1: Visual Romance

1. Lower-end piston-engine planes have carburetors, in which the gasoline is vaporized and mixed with air before combustion. The physics of this process lowers the temperature of the air as it passes through the carburetor. When the engine is operating at

low power, and when the atmospheric humidity is high, the water in the air can turn to ice. This in turn can clog the carburetor, slowing and eventually stopping the engine. Therefore part of prelanding drill on many planes is to turn on the "carb heat" when reducing power for the descent, so that the air stays warm enough to prevent icing.

2.  A stuffier version of the "positive exchange" dialogue would be "I have the controls," followed by "You have the controls."

3.  William Langewiesche, *Inside the Sky: A Meditation on Flight* (New York: Pantheon, 1998), p. 5.

## Chapter 2: The Boys from Baraboo

1.  The authoritative source for general-aviation safety data is the *Nall Report*, published each year by the Aircraft Owners and Pilots Association of Frederick, Maryland. The latest version is available at http://www.aopa.org/asf/publications/.

2.  A fundamental distinction among GA planes is between "piston" and "turbine" engines. Piston planes have internal combustion, piston-driven engines that burn gasoline and turn propellers. Familiar small planes, from the Piper Cub to the Beech Bonanza, have piston engines. Turbine engines are what are generally called "jets." When jet fuel—essentially, kerosene—burns, its combustion products pass through turbine blades and make a rotor turn. If the rotor is connected to propellers, as in the ST50, the plane is a "turboprop." If it doesn't have propellers, it's a "turbine," like all the familiar "jet" airliners. Turbine engines are much more expensive to make but also have fewer moving parts and are vastly more reliable. The difference in their reliability, compared with piston engines, is a main reason why jet-powered planes are safer.

3.  All statistics on general aviation production and shipment are from *1999 GAMA Databook*, General Aviation Manufacturers Association, Washington, D.C.

4.  Rick Durden, "Used Airplanes: Buyer Be Cynical," AvWeb.Com, December 3, 2000. Available at http://www.avweb.com/articles/lounge/tpl0029.html.

5.  Airplane speeds are routinely stated in knots, and distances in nautical miles. A nautical mile equals one "minute" of latitude—that is, one-sixtieth of a degree of latitude—and is about 15 per-

cent longer than the "statute miles" otherwise used in the United States and Britain to measure distances.

## Chapter 3: The GA Mafia

1.  To be more precise: laminar flow involves the passage of a fluid, air or water, over a surface—an airplane wing, a rock in the middle of a stream. This passage always generates friction, which in the airplane's case is undesirable for two reasons: it creates drag, which slows the passage of the plane; and it reduces the lift that the air can provide as it passes over the wing. Researchers discovered that a very thin "boundary layer" of the fluid could, in the right circumstances, pass over the surface with extremely low friction. This is known as "laminar flow." Even in the best circumstances, only a small proportion of a wing's surface can sustain laminar flow. But altering the wing's design and making it as smooth as possible to enhance laminar flow has a very high payoff, because performance improves so dramatically. The flow can be disrupted by extremely small irregularities in a wing's surface—rivet heads, the remains of smashed bugs. So after Cirrus Design used laminar concepts in designing its wing, it also emphasized to its owners that the effort would be wasted unless they routinely washed the wings to get rid of bugs.

2.  See http://www.aero-news.net/news/archive2000/0800news/osh2k1.htm.

3.  Federal Aviation Administration, "Twenty Years of Deregulation: 1978 to 1998," March 29, 2000.

4.  FAA, "Twenty Years of Deregulation."

5.  Jo Thomas, "An Airport Hopes to Build Traffic, Even Just One Flight at a Time," *New York Times*, August 19, 2000.

6.  Holmes compared his airline travel time with that of a direct flight in two different categories of small plane: a fast propeller plane, like a Cirrus or Lancair or Mooney, and a new "Eclipse-class" jet, like the one described in Chapter 7. Trips of 1,000 miles or less were faster in either kind of small plane. All the trips Holmes measured would have been significantly faster in the Eclipse-type small jet.

7.  Holmes elaborated on the point in a presentation called "Life After Airlines," which obviously drew on his own trip-measuring experience: "Today, over a significant mission range, a general

aviation (GA) airplane that cruises at significantly slower speed (~160 knots) can achieve faster average doorstep-to-destination speeds than airliners that actually cruise at much faster speeds (~300 to 600 knots) for hub-spoke routings....For trips less than 1,000 miles, a current GA airplane is faster than the hub-spoke average speed, without taking any benefit at the general aviation destination for proximity to the ultimate destination.... A future GAP-powered GA airplane [one powered by the new engines discussed in Chapter 7] will average as much as one hundred miles per hour faster speed than current GA airplanes. At these speeds, the future GA airplanes will be faster than hub-spoke travel for trips less than about 2,500 miles."

8. Goldin, keynote address, Aircraft Owners..., October 24, 1998.
9. Note that the interstate highway system was not actually completed until the early seventies. Still, the beginning of the system, in the fifties, was the last step forward in travel speed by road.
10. See http://www.aerospace.nasa.gov/home%26home/sats/sld011.htm.
11. In terms of hand-eye coordination and the need for split-second decisions, driving in traffic is far more demanding than normal, noncombat or nonaerobatic airplane flying. Merging into traffic at high speeds, driving on narrow roads with the oncoming traffic clearing by perhaps four feet at combined speed of one hundred miles an hour, scanning for children or pedestrians—these require faster response action than are normally required in an airplane. The real difference in an airplane is that the consequences of a mistake or misjudgment can be so large, plus the fact that at this stage the equipment is so much less reliable, and requires so much extraneous knowledge: about weather, about engine systems (to be sure they don't break), about radio commands, about navigation.

The interesting larger policy point involves not simply the individual skill levels required but those for large-scale public participation. When the first cars were invented, it would have been hard to imagine that essentially all adult members of the public would be expected to operate these vehicles at speeds of seventy miles per hour and upward, in circumstances where a minor loss of attention or steering deviation on a two-way road could lead to a catastrophic head-on collision. Indeed, when cars first appeared, it was thought that only experts, actually called "pilots," would be able to control them. In *The Wind in the Willows*, published in 1908, Mr. Toad's friends try to talk him out of his dangerous determination to drive a car. "It was on them!... The magnificent motor-car, immense, breath-snatching, passionate, with its pilot tense and hugging his wheel, possessed all earth and air for the fraction of a second, flung an enveloping cloud of dust that blinded and enwrapped them utterly."

12. Goldin, keynote address, Aircraft Owners..., October 24, 1998.

13. The existing small-plane fleet averaged 150 miles per hour; that speed should be doubled, Goldin said, then tripled. Attaining that goal in turn required progress toward significantly new engine designs, since today's piston engines could attain higher speeds only through costly, heavy, brute-force application of extra horsepower. The typical piston engine had a "Time Between Overhaul" of 1,600 flying hours. This meant that the typical small plane, in the air for 250 to 300 hours a year, needed essentially to be rebuilt every five or six years. This was very much like cars in the fifties; NASA's goal was to make new airplanes as reliable and low-maintenance as 2000-era cars, which are now manufactured to go 100,000 miles without major problems or need for major servicing. Translated to aviation, the target was roughly ten years of heavy-duty flying before the need for overhaul. The engines used in small airplanes are not tremendously larger than those of cars—a typical one is under 200 horsepower, and a big one is 300—but they are much noisier and more polluting. Automobile-level environmental impact was the next goal. Bureaucratic approval for any change in aircraft design was almost as slow as the procedure for approving new drugs. Goldin said that the typical approval period should be cut by 75 percent, from two years to six months, and that the cost for meeting the certification standards should be reduced by 90 percent.

Perhaps most important, NASA concluded, all elements of the price of small-plane flying had to come down. New small airplanes generally cost between fifty and one hundred dollars per pound. New cars cost about ten dollars. Airplanes will always cost more per pound, since they have a stronger incentive than cars to pack more value into less weight, but twenty-five dollars or lower could be a goal. Goldin suggested fifteen. Small planes in 2000 cost roughly $1,000 for each mile-per-hour of top speed—those capable of going 200 miles-per-hour cost at least $200,000. The price of speed in even nice cars is only about one-third as great: a fancy car that goes eighty miles per hour would cost not $80,000 but $25,000 to $40,000. Electronic equipment was a major cost component in aviation; why shouldn't its price fall every two years just as it had in the computer and Internet world? The handheld GPS systems sold to hikers and campers were functionally very similar to those in airplane panels, but cost roughly one-sixth as much.

14. "Goldin Defends NASA Role in Aviation," *AOPA Flight Training*, October 2000, p. 12.

15. See http://www.aero-news.net/news/archive2000/0800news/osh2k1.htm.

**Chapter 4: The Teardrop and the Cigar Tube**

1. An additional weight problem comes up in FAA certification. A defect-free wing or spar made of fiberglass would start out being heavier than a comparable defect-free aluminum part. Moreover, it is harder to be sure that the fiberglass was free of defects than it is to make the same determination about aluminum. Most defects in a metal surface are easy to spot on visual inspection or with X rays. But the defects that can make fiberglass weak are hard to find. Mainly they involve places where two layers of fiberglass did not completely bond, and there is no easy way to tell that from outside or by X-ray. Therefore FAA regulations require composite airplanes to be built extra thick (which means extra heavy), so that even if there are hidden defects the plane will be strong enough.

2. Among those responsible for hashing out the plane's design in these battles were Gary Poelma, who worked on the wing; Don Kitson and Mike Lenz, on the control surfaces; Dave Rathbun, on the wing and wing systems; Jeff Knutson, on "firewall forward," which meant the engine compartment of the plane; Marcel LaFond, on fuselage support, console, and interior support; Dick Showalter, Paul Brey, Jay Yeakle, and Doug Lee on structural analysis, and Hal Fletcher on structural testing. Steve Serfling, Brian Janzig, and Greg Crawford worked on the electrical system and avionics. And the flight test and engineering team

included Scott Anderson, Snorri Gudmunsson, Gary Black, and Mike Stevens.

3.  Unlike a steering wheel, an airplane's yoke must go through a substantial range of fore-and-aft movement. To point the nose of the plane up, the pilot pulls the yoke close toward his chest. To point the nose down, he pushes it forward. The person in the right-side passenger/copilot seat must be careful not to jostle the yoke in front of him, which is linked to the one the pilot controls, or interfere with its movements when the pilot turns or pulls it back. In most phases of flight a pilot (unlike a car driver) touches only one small part of the control yoke. As the pilot sits in the left seat, his right hand is usually occupied with things other than steering the plane. Operating the throttle, raising and lowering the flaps, tuning the radios, lowering the landing gear—the controls for these and other chores are all conveniently placed between the pilot's and copilot's seat, accessible to the pilot's right hand. As a result people learn to fly one-handed, with their left hand holding the left side of the control yoke. In the busiest portions of a flight—takeoff, approach and landing, intercepting navigational signals for changes in course—the pilot virtually always has his right hand occupied with the throttle, the flaps, the radio, the settings on the autopilot. What would seem to be the "hard" part of aircraft control, guiding the plane right and left to keep the correct course, and up and down to the correct altitude, especially when gliding in for landing, is thus the sole responsibility of the left hand, for right- and left-handers alike. Except if the pilot is flying a fighter plane, in which case he uses a control stick with his right hand. This all seems to be a great lesson in human adaptability. Most pilots are, of course, right-handed and in the abstract would probably think that they would need their dominant hand for the finesse work of steering and landing. In reality everyone gets used to left-handed operation early in the process.

## Chapter 5: The Plane with the Parachute

1.  William Langewiesche, *Inside the Sky.* The analysis of the crash was first published as "The Lessons of ValuJet 592," by William Langewiesche, *The Atlantic Monthly* (March, 1998).
2.  The idea that if a pilot can no longer see the ground or level hori-

zon, he will *inevitably* lose control of the plane and enter a spin-ning descent—unless he has been specially trained in "instrument flying" techniques—is one of the hardest concepts to accept in aviation. The best explanation of why this is so is in William Langewiesche's "The Turn," published first in *The Atlantic Monthly* (December, 1993) and later as part of his *Inside the Sky* (1998).

3. *1999 Nall Report: Accident Trends and Factors for 1998*, Frederick, Maryland: Air Safety Foundation. Available at http://www.aopa.org/asf/publications/99nall.html

4. All of these from U.S. Department of Transportation, *Transportation Statistics Annual Report 1999*, available at http://www.bts.gov/transtu/tsar/tsar1999/tables/04tab2.htm.

5. Such accidents usually occur because a crankshaft breaks or the engine stops for some other reason; or, more frequently, when a "vacuum-pump system" fails. A sudden engine failure is most dangerous when a single-engine plane is flying at night or in the clouds over hostile terrain, or when one engine of a twin-engine plane fails when the plane is trying to take off. The resulting imbalanced thrust can make it impossible to control the plane. The vacuum pumps power the gyroscopes, which in turn permit a pilot to know whether he is flying straight and level while in the clouds. A vacuum or gyro failure, unlike a stopped engine, does not directly cause the plane to come down. Indeed, instru-ment-rated pilots are trained in "partial panel" techniques, which in theory let them guide the plane safely even if the vacuum-driven gyros have failed. But it can be the first step in a chain of events leading to an accident, as a pilot becomes disoriented in the clouds, gets further and further "behind the plane," and lets the plane enter a spinning descent.

6. Senator John Heinz, of Pennsylvania, died in a small-plane crash in 1991. As the plane neared an airport for landing, the pilot couldn't be sure whether the landing gear had gone down. As is common in this situation, he flew by the airport's control tower and asked the controllers to see if they could tell whether the wheels were down. While making this pass, the plane ran into a helicopter.

7. The most important other change was removing the "prop" con-trol. After receiving their initial private-pilot certificate, aspiring flyers are usually next certified to handle "complex" airplanes.

These are defined as planes with retractable landing gear, and with a way to control the "pitch" of the propeller. A plane can work most efficiently if the angle at which the propeller bites through the air can change in different phases of flight. The propeller works best if it can take relatively shallow bites through the air when the airplane is going slowly, for example on takeoff or in a steep climb. This is comparable to the function of low gear in a car or bike. Then, when the plane is cruising or descending, the propeller is most efficient if it can take a deeper bite of air per rotation, as with high gear in a car or bike.

In "complex" planes, the pilot controls the propeller's angle with a lever or knob. The Cirrus designers decided to take this control away and make the adjustments automatic; in effect, they were installing an automatic transmission in the airplane. "This is something I just never have to think about again," says Alan Klapmeier. "If I don't really have to do anything about it, why give me a reason to worry about it." As with automatic transmission, there is some small loss in theoretical maximum efficiency; the company reasoned that the gain in simplicity would be worthwhile.

8.  The best explanation of stalls, and most other aspects of the physics of flight, is in Wolfgang Langewiesche's *Stick and Rudder: An Explanation of the Art of Flying* (New York: McGraw Hill, 1976).

9.  In normal flying circumstances, a pilot would correct a plane's descent by pulling the nose up, and would correct an unwanted turn to left or right by using the ailerons to move the wings the opposite way. The ailerons have no effect in a spin, and pulling the nose up only makes things worse, by tightening and accelerating the spiral. When pilots receive spin training, they learn a counterintuitive series of steps. These begin by using the rudder to stop the spiral, and then by pointing the nose of the plane— which at that moment is headed for the ground—even farther down, to ensure a fast flow of air over the wings to end the stall.

10. On its website (http://209.238.147.86/BRS21.html) the company kept a list of lives saved in the crashes. Through late 2000 there were more than 130 such saves, from altitudes as high as 11,000 feet and as low as less than 200.

11. On various aviation websites and at conferences, this argument raged, driven mainly by disputes about the different kinds of

velocity the chute was designed to absorb. Once the chute was
fully expanded, the plane would fall—and hit the ground—at a
speed as high as seventeen miles per hour, or more than 1,500
feet per minute. This is, again, comparable to a ten-foot straight
drop, and it is a much higher vertical speed than a pilot could
expect in a controlled glide. With the engine out, a typical small
plane can glide at a descent rate of 500 feet per minute, which is
slow enough to manage a normal landing. Therefore, the argument went, since a plane falling beneath its parachute would
come down three times faster than one under its pilot's control,
why even consider the parachute option?

One reply was: *if* the pilot has the choice for a power-off glide
to a reasonable landing area, then that's the choice most pilots
will make. But sometimes that choice doesn't exist: if the plane is
in clouds and the pilot doesn't know where the ground is; if it's
nighttime over the mountains, and the pilot can't see what he
would be hitting; and so on.

The larger reply is that the comparison of descent speeds is
misleading. When a vehicle comes to a sudden stop, the energy
that must be dissipated—that is, the potential for damaging the
vehicle and its occupants—rises with the square of the vehicle's
total velocity. A plane dropping at 1,500 feet per minute will
have nine times the energy to be dissipated on impact as one
falling at 500 feet per minute.

That would seem to make the controlled glide so much better
an alternative to the parachute as to raise doubts about the parachute's worth at all. The problem is that "vertical energy"—the
speed at which the plane is falling toward earth—is only one
component of the energy in a crash. The other part is the vehicle's "horizontal energy"—how fast it is moving forward, across
the ground. After all, in most automobile crashes, the "vertical
velocity" is zero, but the cars can inflict or absorb tremendous
damage if their horizontal velocity goes from eighty miles per
hour to zero in a collision with an obstacle or another car. Even
for airplanes, the sudden change in horizontal velocity can be
what does the gravest damage. The total velocity of a plane in a
nose dive, straight down, is nearly all made of its vertical velocity. But a plane whose engine has failed, and that glides into
trees or hills with a vertical velocity of only five to ten miles an

hour but a forward velocity of one hundred miles per hour or more may suffer severe damage, as a car would.

The reduction in horizontal—not just vertical—velocity turns out to be the most important contribution of the parachute in many cases. Once the chute is deployed, the plane has no independent horizontal velocity. It is being carried by the wind, like an untethered balloon, and has only the horizontal velocity relative to the ground that the wind does. Its total velocity is the fifteen miles per hour of descent plus the wind's speed over the ground. This will almost always be less than that of a plane in a glide, whose vertical velocity may be only five to ten miles an hour but whose horizontal velocity will be around eighty miles per hour. And because of the principle that damage varies with the square of preimpact velocity, the expected total risk for the plane with a chute is also much lower.

## Chapter 6: What Makes an Airplane Fly

1. http://www.avweb.com/newswire/news9913.html.
2. As it happens, I had seen a Cirrus airplane for the first time on March 22, 1999. I had been reading about the company for several years, and I heard that a demo model would be arriving at Boeing Field, in Seattle, that day. With a friend, I went up for an hour's flight, conducted by one of the company pilots. I was charmed—but when I heard the very next day about the crash I said to my wife, "Too bad. That's the end of these guys."
3. As one aviation report said afterwards, "Static testing on other Cirrus SR20 prototypes revealed that it is possible for the leading edge of the right aileron to become jammed against the wing when the aileron is deflected downward and the wing is flexed upward to its maximum design limit. The gap tolerance between the aileron and wing are critical factors in determining the potential for jamming. So long as Scott kept the power up and pushed down on the yoke with all of his body weight, he was able to maintain relative control." *Midwest Flyer* magazine, December 1999/January 2000.
4. For the younger readers in the audience: In 1937 the German dirigible *Hindenberg*, the largest flying machine of its time, exploded in flames while it was a few hundred feet above the

airport in Lakehurst, New Jersey. The hydrogen that was used to fill the *Hindenberg* burned so quickly that in less than one minute the ship had been burned up and most of the sixty-plus people aboard had died. Huge airships like the *Hindenberg* had been popular long-haul transport vehicles until then, but never afterwards.

5. John Kenneth Galbraith, *The Nature of Mass Poverty* (Cambridge, Mass.: Harvard University Press, 1980).

6. This included an outright grant of $229,000 to build the new factory; proceeds of two bonds totaling over $1.4 million to finance the construction; and other concessions for rent and training costs.

7. Cirrus's critics in the aircraft business say that the Klapmeiers' main mistake has been their consistent underestimation of how much it would cost to get their airplane built, designed, certified, and into mass production. By late 2000, after all, the company had spent some $85 million, not the $10 million that was its original target. "We weren't really off in our estimates by $75 million," Alan Klapmeier says. "But we naively thought that if we had $10 million in equity, banks and development companies would let us get the rest. We know that $10 million would not have been enough. But $20 million in equity should have been, if we could have gotten the other financing in time."

8. For example, "Cirrus intends to focus its products on all levels of personal aircraft transportation. Between the introductory product represented by the low-cost SR20 and the ST50 turboprop business airplane is a wide range of aircraft for general aviation.... Management believes the success of the business beyond the five-year plan period includes product line expansion and future generations of innovative aircraft."

9. The "award" article said, "On paper, the SR20 isn't much faster than current offerings, carries about the same payload.... So why the big deal?

   "Because the SR20 subtly advances the state of general aviation technology across several fronts, with incremental improvements that have, thus far at least, proven practical and affordable. It looks different too, sleek and sexy, not boxy and stodgy.... It's too soon to say if Cirrus Design has invented the airplane company of the future, but so far they're on the right track." *Aviation Consumer*, August, 2000, pp. 9–10.

10. In the online publication AvWeb, with a wide following among pilots, the writer Dave Higdon reviewed several new planes. He liked all of them but had this to say about the Cirrus: "Not only does the SR20 stand out because of its parachute, it also stands out because of its size, its comfort, its equipment and its value. Add in the parachute, the composites, the moving map, the avionics, and the airplane's value really stands out. ...In my view, Cirrus created the best-handling, best-harmonized flying machine to come along since the Bonanza—for decades a benchmark for gauging the handling and harmony of single-engine airplanes. The SR20 nearly matches Walter Beech's classic, benchmark design in overall performance—for less than one-third the money." Dave Higdon, "Plastic Planes Part Two," AvWeb, Fall 2000. Available at http://www.avweb.com/articles/cirrussr20/.

## Chapter 7: Disruptive Technology

1. The city is named for a nearby lake, which in turn was called "Walled Lake" because of a stone wall running along its shores. The wall was built in the era before white settlement of the region.

2. The navigation improvements came in two mutually reinforcing stages. During most of its mission, the cruise missile is guided by signals from the Global Positioning System satellite network. Constant improvements in the speed and reliability of small computers made this initial stage of the navigation more and more reliable. Then, as the cruise missile nears its destination, its onboard computers match its readings of the terrain over which it is passing with internally stored maps of the target zone. This stage, too, became more practical and reliable with faster computers.

3. A turbojet gets its thrust by shooting exhaust out the back at high speed. A turbofan uses part of the energy of combustion to turn a large fan at the front of the engine. This drives some additional air backwards; as this air leaves the rear of the engine, it creates additional thrust, even though it was not involved in combustion. The ratio between this extra, fan-driven airflow and the flow of combustion products is known as the "bypass ratio."

The higher the bypass ratio, the more efficient the turbofan in generating thrust from a certain amount of fuel.

4. The military did keep alive a variant of the flying belt: a device that looked like a rocket-powered pulpit. Jet exhaust pointing straight down would power the craft, and the pilot would steer it by leaning his body weight forward, back, or to the side. A model of the device is on display at Williams's corporate headquarters.

5. House Committee on Transportation and Infrastructure, Aviation Subcommittee, *The Future of Aviation Technology*, 106th Cong., 2nd. sess., May 16, 2000. Available at http://www.house.gov/transportation/aviation/05–16–00/williams.html.

6. In his congressional testimony, Williams explained the development thus: "To demonstrate the possibilities that the FJX engine could create, we designed a six-passenger, twin-engine, general aviation prototype aircraft we called the V-Jet." The plane would cost roughly as much as existing piston planes, but it would perform like the costly jets. "We quietly kept working on the engine and aircraft design for a few years."

7. In training the engine usually "recovers" miraculously as the plane nears the ground and the instructor pushes the throttle back in. Unless, that is, the drill is being held near an airport, in which case the pilot is expected to glide the plane all the way in to a landing on the runway. A power-off glide to a landing at Carroll County Airport, outside Washington, D.C., was one of the highlights of my "check ride" for a private pilot's certificate.

8. Diesel engines run on the same fuel as jet engines. Although heavier than gas engines, they have fewer parts and are more reliable. They also use fuel more efficiently in most flight conditions. To speed the development of affordable, modernized diesel engines, GAP held a competition for the best proposal for new diesel designs. In 1996, Holmes's GAP program awarded a $9.5 million contract to Lycoming, one of the two dominant piston engine makers (the other is Teledyne Continental) to build a better diesel. The terms of the contract were to create an engine that sold for half as much as existing models; that used only 75 percent as much fuel; that lasted 75 percent longer between overhauls; and that was significantly quieter and less polluting.

9. See http://www.grc.nasa.gov/WWW/AST/GAP/.

10. Williams said of the arrangement, "NASA's goal was to have the

engine industry compete for a technology advancement program in which NASA would provide 50 percent of the funding. Dan Goldin's vision was that such a program could revitalize our sagging general aviation industry sales with new technology engines." House Committee, *The Future of Aviation Technology*.

11. On a normal map Seattle looks as if it is farther from Chicago than San Francisco is. Actually, it's about one hundred miles closer.

12. Friction-stir technology was developed and patented by the TWI Corporation, based in Cambridge, England. Full details on how the system works are available at http://www.twi.co.uk/bestprac/datashts/fswintro.html.

## Epilogue

1. Extensive information about SATS is available at http://sats.nasa.gov.

2. Extensive information about the FAA's Free Flight programs is at http://ffp1.faa.gov/home/home.asp.

# About the Author

James Fallows is the National Correspondent for *The Atlantic Monthly*, where he has worked for more than twenty years. He has written frequently for other publications, including the *New York Review of Books*, *Slate*, and *The Industry Standard*, and has been a regular commentator for National Public Radio. His previous books include *Breaking the News* and *National Defense*. He has worked as a presidential speechwriter, the editor of *U.S News & World Report*, and a consultant at Microsoft in software design, and has taught journalism at the University of California, Berkeley. He is an instrument-rated pilot. He and his wife have two sons and live in Berkeley, California. His website is www.JamesFallows.com.

# Index

PublicAffairs is a new nonfiction publishing house and a tribute to the standards, values, and flair of three persons who have served as mentors to countless reporters, writers, editors, and book people of all kinds, including me.

I. F. STONE, proprietor of *I. F. Stone's Weekly*, combined a commitment to the First Amendment with entrepreneurial zeal and reporting skill and became one of the great independent journalists in American history. At the age of eighty, Izzy published *The Trial of Socrates*, which was a national bestseller. He wrote the book after he taught himself ancient Greek.

BENJAMIN C. BRADLEE was for nearly thirty years the charismatic editorial leader of *The Washington Post*. It was Ben who gave the *Post* the range and courage to pursue such historic issues as Watergate. He supported his reporters with a tenacity that made them fearless and it is no accident that so many became authors of influential, best-selling books.

ROBERT L. BERNSTEIN, the chief executive of Random House for more than a quarter century, guided one of the nation's premier publishing houses. Bob was personally responsible for many books of political dissent and argument that challenged tyranny around the globe. He is also the founder and longtime chair of Human Rights Watch, one of the most respected human rights organizations in the world.

For fifty years, the banner of Public Affairs Press was carried by its owner, Morris B. Schnapper, who published Gandhi, Nasser, Toynbee, Truman, and about 1,500 other authors. In 1983, Schnapper was described by *The Washington Post* as "a redoubtable gadfly." His legacy will endure in the books to come.

Peter Osnos, *Publisher*